STUDY SKILLS FOR MANAGERS

STUDY SKILLS
FOR
MANAGERS

BILL MAYON-WHITE

P·C·P

Paul Chapman
Publishing Ltd

Copyright © 1990 Bill Mayon-White

First published 1990

Paul Chapman Publishing Ltd
144 Liverpool Road
London N1 1LA

British Library Cataloguing in Publication Data
Mayon-White, Bill
   Study skills for managers.
   1. Managers. Self-development
   I. Title
   658.409

ISBN 1 85396 088 8

Typeset by DP Photosetting, Aylesbury, Bucks
Printed and bound by
Athenaeum Press Ltd, Gateshead, Tyne & Wear.

FGH   987

Contents

Preface

Any manager looking ahead to the 1990s will be aware of the increasing rate of change of contemporary organizational life. Increasing competitive pressures in the 1980s started a trend which now continues apace. Information technology is still causing major changes to the office environment. Other systems based on the same technology are also changing the factory as computer controls for machine tools and process plant revolutionize all areas of industrial life. Robots in the factory and the computer network in the office are but two of the dimensions of change which must be met by today's managers.

Other important changes have taken place in the human side of organizational life. Old-style autocratic structures are giving way to more open and flexible ways of working which reflect a shift in values and attitudes in the workplace. Some of these changes have been driven by legislation, but most reflect our changing expectations of 'job' and 'work'. The hours of work have been reduced, while incomes have grown, with the result that many of us enjoy greater leisure and a higher quality of life than our parents' generation. But simultaneously there is growing awareness of stress in the workplace and a concern for the implications of a fast-moving and fast-changing world for the individual and for society.

Not all the changes can be viewed as beneficial in the short run for in the early years of the decade the run down of non-competitive concerns and of manufacturing industry in particular had a high cost in the human currency of lost jobs and unemployment. An economic policy which aimed to increase competition had the effect of increasing unemployment. This in turn saw the introduction of new agencies such as the Training Agency (formerly the Manpower Services Commission) with a brief to retrain and reskill. The continued and growing interest in management education can also be seen as another delayed, but inevitable consequence of this restructuring.

The task of coping with change must start with an acceptance that new knowledge and skills will have to be acquired, not once but several times during a working life. The concept of lifelong learning is no longer the sole province of bodies such as the Open University which specialize in distance learning for adults. The idea of self-directed or open learning now has widespread support and enjoys the endorsement of both government and industry. Schools, colleges, training agencies and management development specialists within companies have always recognized the vital contribution that training and education can make to motivation and performance, but never before have training and education been so highly valued by society at large.

A manager has several sources of support for his or her development – family, friends, colleagues, as well as the professional adviser and trainer – but the trend is towards individual responsibility for self-development. This book is intended to provide you, the reader, with some practical help in this task.

Anyone picking up a book which aims to be a handbook or guide relies on the author for clear unambiguous prose which is both stimulating and interesting. Thus there is a special challenge facing an author setting out to provide advice and help to managers on self-development, study skills, reading and the preparation of written reports. Can I practise what I preach? As the reader you will judge whether or not the ideas in this book have been conveyed in a clear and helpful fashion.

Self-development is still a relatively new term: the concept is still evolving and being refined, and other authors have written about study skills for the younger university or college student. By bringing the two strands of study skills and self-development together in one book I have attempted to synthesize a selection of material which will prove effective and stimulating for any manager at any stage in his or her career. Any selection will be eclectic, but where I have missed the target or where there are shortcomings then, of course, the fault is mine.

The material in this book is derived from more than a decade of teaching adults in face-to-face settings and through distance learning. Whatever their reasons for study and whatever their previous educational experience, such students bring to their studies a wealth of knowledge, and yet all face similar problems in getting started in their courses. If the chapters which follow help you and show that self-development can be fun and stimulating my task has been worthwhile.

Acknowledgements

With any project of this kind my job as an author would have been much more difficult were it not for the help and advice of those who were prepared to read and comment on a series of drafts.

Most important has been the feedback from Open University students over the years: in tutorials, at our summer schools and residential courses. Their comments and reactions have pointed the way towards the study skills discussed in these pages.

My thanks go to the following organizations and individuals for permission to include material in this book. To London Transport Limited for permission to include in Chapter 4 the diagram of the London Underground System. To Geoffrey Hancock for permission to include in Chapter 5 his article 'Quality brings sales dividends to Jaguar'. To Professor The Revd Jack Mahoney SJ, Director, King's College Business Ethics Research Centre, London for permission to include in Chapter 5 extracts from his article 'Morality at boardroom level'. To Her Majesty's Stationery Office for permission to include in Chapter 7 the diagram 7.1 on coping with stress.

Special thanks must go to Sarah Brunner, Eileen Scholes and Sandy Taylor: all three were involved as clients for an earlier project for a study pack for managers who were starting out on courses designed to give them the opportunity to progress to an MBA degree if they wished. That study pack preceded and gave rise to this book. Rosemary Smith of the Open Business School gave me useful feedback and comments on the penultimate draft and Marianne Lagrange of Paul Chapman Publishing encouraged and supported me through the difficulties which accompany any writing project.

Most patient of all were my wife Joyce and our two daughters Elaine and Rhian, who responded to the inevitable interrupted weekends and late-night writing stints with cheerful good humour.

IBM and Filofax are registered trade marks.

Bill Mayon-White
London.
September 1989

Introduction:
Management Education and this Book

This book has been designed as a starting point for any manager who wishes to tackle his or her own 'self-development' or to return to more formal study after some years away from school, college or university.

During the last few years two studies, one by Charles Handy and the other by John Constable and Roger McCormick (1987), have had a major impact on management education. Both reports addressed the lack of provision for managers in the United Kingdom and made suggestions for improvements. Perhaps the most important contribution made by these studies has been to provide a focus for debate and to draw attention to the major issues.

One of these issues is the relatively small proportion of managers receiving training of any kind. Thus Constable and McCormick (1987) estimate that of some 130,000 entrants to 'management' in any year about 90,000 might be expected to have 'serious management responsibilities'. Their report (1987) then states that 'most of the 90,000 new managers-to-be will receive either no formal introduction to the elements of business or will wait until mid-career at which stage over one-third will still receive nothing'.

One direct result of these studies has been the formation of a partnership between industry and educators in the form of the Council for Management Education, and progress is being made to reorganize and extend the provision of management education and to rationalize management qualifications.

One outcome of this initiative is certain; a growing level of participation in management education by people of all ages. There is a link between management skills and the study skills which are the subject of this book. For example, time management is a skill which is common to both and its application in either field will have benefits for the other. Communication skills, both verbal and written, are also common to both and it matters little whether these are acquired or refined under the heading of 'management' or 'study' skills. Indeed at the core of the concept of self-development is the maxim: 'Manager manage yourself!'

This book is designed to build on these links and through study skills lead to improved management performance. You should find that it is a useful source of help and advice which will allow you to acquire new skills. It is intended to be a practical rather than comprehensive guide to self-development and study skills.

The research into learning skills is a huge but diffuse field, ranging from studies of the relationships between mothers and children to neurophysiology. This book does not attempt to link study skills to research; indeed it could be argued that many of the links are tenuous and overstretched in some study skills texts. Instead the focus is on techniques which students have found to work in practice.

The book is arranged to cover self-development and learning skills. The topics include the mind and memory, information management, and those key study skills – reading, writing and critical analysis.

Each chapter discusses particular techniques and ideas, and contains exercises designed to give you some confidence in your own ability to put the skills to work. The exercises are included in the body of the book, and while a 'skim read' is a good way to discover the structure and range of the material, you should allow sufficient time to work through each exercise. This will ensure that you develop a set of practical skills and not just a superficial appreciation of the learning process.

Wherever possible the text gives suggested time limits for individual exercises. Take them seriously as you work through the material for the first time. Later, if you have the opportunity, return and pursue in greater detail those activities which hold most interest for you.

In some cases the exercises require you to complete a table, on occasion these exercises are of a kind which can usefully be repeated at intervals in order to see if you have changed your views or improved your skill levels. Where this is so there is an invitation in the text suggesting that you photocopy the blank table before proceeding. But this advice is unhelpful if you turn to an exercise in the course of a train journey! So the invitation is first made here. Skim read the book and make a note of any tables within exercises which you may like to re-use. Photocopy these now.

Suggestions for further reading are included by way of reference, but the book is self-contained. To achieve the study objectives set out in Chapter 1 you need look no further than the material in this book. If you decide to use it as a study text in a somewhat more formal manner, then allocate no more than about twelve hours spread over one or two weeks. There will be some variation in the study time and work patterns of individuals but you should treat this as a target and plan accordingly.

1

Self-Development and the Return to Learning: Where Are You Now?

You and your career

Trends and fashions influence every aspect of life, and the apparently mundane world of training and personnel management is no exception. Over recent years human resources managers have replaced personnel managers and for managers training has become 'self-development' and 'management development'. However, these new titles are more than mere cosmetic changes in name. They reflect a subtle but important shift in emphasis. Workers and staff are no longer units of resource, but have become 'people'!

Tom Peters, the American management guru, drew attention to this in one of his television lectures by citing the all too familiar example of British (and American) company annual reports in which the chairman and directors are named, but which fail to name any other staff shown in glossy photographs of factories, offices and products. It is encouraging to note that he was also able to report improvements and to mention companies whose publications did refer to all staff by name.

In the new climate you and your colleagues have become individuals; people to be retained and encouraged to develop within the organization. Employees can now be seen as people with legitimate aspirations and energies which, if directed and focused, can yield benefits for the employing organization and for the individual. (Does your company match up to this image? Do you as a manager match up to its ideals?)

You will fit somewhere into this pattern though your own organization may not (yet!) have achieved the paradise suggested above. Whatever your job and whatever your age or aspirations there will always be something new and useful to learn. Of course the choice will depend on the industry in which you work, and on your role and experience, but in choosing any course of study you should be aiming for something which benefits you and your employer. After all, unless your studies are to be only a hobby or leisure pursuit they should improve your performance at work and help your career.

Building commitment

The start of any new activity almost always generates some feelings of uncertainty and concern. Returning to study is no different in this respect but for many people the prospect is made more difficult by memories of school and college.

Whatever image you portray to the world at large, be it that of a self-confident, outgoing sort of person or a quieter, more introspective one, you are very likely to have some misgivings about starting to study again, particularly if several years have elapsed since you last undertook any structured programme of study.

For many people the idea of studying as an adult, when perhaps they already have children at school or college, is a curious one. After all, if you are trained or have experience in a particular field or profession why should study or retraining be necessary? Yet, over a typical working life of thirty-five to forty years, a whole series of technologies, laws, products and practices will come and go. Without further training we are all ill-equipped to take advantage of such changes, or indeed to cope with them and maintain ourselves as happy, healthy individuals capable of contributing effectively to the organizations of the 1990s.

Exercise 1.1

Look at your own working life and consider the impact of just two areas of change - computing and communications - on work patterns and skills.

First, make a list of changes which you have experienced as a result of, say, the introduction of computers and improved communications technology in your place of work and, second, prepare a matching list of the skills which you and others have had to acquire or still need to acquire.

Changes in my office/ factory to do with computing	New skills needed (and by whom)
E.g. word processing	Computer use by secretaries and managers

1
2
3
4
5
Etc.

Changes in my office/ factory to do with communications	Skills needed (and by whom)

E.g. fax and telex machines

1
2
3
4
5
Etc.

Now repeat the exercise, but this time put yourself in the place of your parents or grandparents. Choose a simple example such as the adding machine, typewriter, or even the ballpoint pen.

Changes in my office/ factory to do with computing	New skills needed (and by whom)

E.g. the adding machine

1
2
3
4
5
Etc.

Changes in my office/   *Skills needed (and by whom)*
factory to do with
communications

E.g. the telephone

1
2
3
4
5
Etc.

Compare your lists with those which might have been prepared by your parents or grandparents for the same two activities. You will immediately find that one activity, computing, didn't exist twenty-five years ago in the sense of today's use of the term.

(Use examples of other changes if you prefer, or if you cannot think of suitable examples in the two suggested categories.)

Your answer to Exercise 1.1 should demonstrate that we all must face up to skill changes in the course of working life and therefore to the need for continuous updating and retraining. For the practising manager training provides not only new skills but also the opportunity to reflect on one's own performance and to share ideas about the process of managing with a peer group.

In the United Kingdom, only over the last few years have we gradually come to recognize the vital role that training and management education can play in giving companies a competitive edge and the flexibility to cope with new challenges. Many commentators claim that other countries, such as the United States, Germany and Japan, are far ahead of the United Kingdom in this respect. For example, Handy (1987) concludes that managers in those countries are more likely to have higher qualifications than their British counterparts and that they have already understood and adopted the idea of self-development. Some recent studies have shown that by certain yardsticks productivity in a number of British manufacturing companies is now moving ahead of our competitors (for example in the motor industry) but it must be recognized that these same concerns have undergone major reorganization in the last decade.

In discussions about management education it is sometimes argued that employees tend to focus too much on the value of qualifications while employers tend to discount their importance and instead emphasize the value of experience. A national structure for management qualifications is presently being discussed. A stepwise design starting with a certificate and moving to diploma and the MBA degree has been proposed. There is also a need to consider the role of qualifications in Europe as we approach 1992 and the single market. Will further study and an appropriate qualification lead you to a better job in a unified market? The purpose of this stepwise design for management qualification in the United Kingdom is to enable you to gain practical skills in marketing, finance, human resources, etc., and then, if you wish, to proceed towards a higher qualification.

Many management students find that the support provided by a structured programme of study such as a part- or full-time MBA is a powerful incentive to overcome any resistance to learning. In this respect a formal programme must be more directed and effective than a one-off short course. This conclusion is borne out by the high demand for the part-time MBAs offered by some business schools.

Even more important is the experience of working alongside other adult students, which can lead to the discovery that learning can be fun and stimulating whatever the field of study. New horizons are opened up and new views on life emerge from the peer group debates and discussions which accompany any educational process.

'Continuing education' is the label now used for the expanding field of lifelong learning. (The terms 'continuing education', 'distance learning' and 'open learning' are easily confused. Continuing education is best used for lifelong learning, distance learning implies remote delivery (coupled to open access with the Open University undergraduate programme), while open learning implies open access, for both local and remote provision.) Gone is the time when apprenticeships were thought to equip people with the skills needed for an entire working life. Instead there is now the opportunity and need to undertake many forms of study and self-development in order to acquire new skills. Under these circumstances the label of 'mature student' has become almost irrelevant as people of all ages enrol for classes and courses, ranging from the short company-based training event to part-time postgraduate study in universities and polytechnics. Innovations such as the Open University, with its huge student numbers, have given a meaning and focus to the idea of continuing education since its establishment in 1969. Companies and government bodies such as the Training Agency are now paying much more attention to training. At last it is being recognized that people are the most important asset of any organization with the result that training and updating are now viewed as a form of investment in people. New forms of education have been developed, with self-study books and texts such as this becoming more popular.

Whether studying independently or in the more formal setting of a college or university you will face several challenges. Two of these are especially important: the need to gain self-confidence in your own learning skills and abilities; and to achieve an integration between study, work and your social life.

The aims of this book

The skills taught in this book will not only help you in your studies, but also apply directly to your everyday work. You will get an immediate return on the time invested in working with the ideas in this book.

Consider the aims in Table 1.1 carefully. You will need to match them to your own particular study goals.

Table 1.1   The aims of study skills for managers

A   To enable you, a busy manager with a demanding professional life, to identify ways of integrating study with work and to resolve any conflicting demands on your time which a new task may generate.

B   To enable you to make an initial assessment of your own strengths and weaknesses and training needs as a manager.

C   To enable you to acquire and develop a range of study skills and an understanding of the principles which are the basis of memory, reading and critical analysis.

D   To enable you to apply the skills taught and thus reinforce them through application and practice.

E   To encourage you to develop a pattern of study which fits your own lifestyle and makes full use of available learning resources.

F   To understand and use self-help groups and peer-group support.

Exercise 1.2

Spend about five minutes thinking about the aims in Table 1.1 as they apply to you, and then try to grade them against your own study skills. Rank your own skills as high, medium or low against each of the five aims, using the grid below, and add comments on your own assessment of the areas where you might improve your skill levels.

Your ranking of your skill levels in relation to each of the aims A to F

	High	Medium	Low
Aim A Integrate study (or other activity) with work			
Aim B Assess your own training needs			
Aim C Acquire study skills			
Aim D Apply new skills			
Aim E Develop a study pattern or habit			
Aim F Understand and make use of peer-group support			

The range of study skills

We now turn to the range of study skills which are dealt with in more detail in the later chapters of this book. In the exercises which follow you will be asked to look more carefully at the different skills used in the day-to-day business of management, and in the business of study.

Exercise 1.3

Make a list of the skills which you draw on when, say, preparing a business report. Continue to add skills as you think of them, e.g. planning, critical reading, collection and analysis of data, etc.

Skills which you use in report-writing:

1.
2.
3.

4

5.

Etc.

What further skills might you use in preparing an oral presentation of your report to a group of colleagues?

The skills dealt with in this book will almost certainly include some of those which you have listed. Some typical management functions, e.g. report-writing, demand skills which overlap with those required for study. These study skills are considered below against the course aims presented above. Figure 1.1 sets these out as a grid in which individual skills have been grouped under four headings. The grid shows that most of these contribute to more than one of the aims.

The four broad headings of reading, self-development, memory

Aims	Study skills			
	1 Reading	2 Self-development	3 Memory	4 Writing
Aim A Integrate study (or other activity) with work	Yes	Yes		Yes
Aim B Assess your training needs	Yes		Yes	
Aim C Acquire study skills		Yes		
Aim D Apply new skills	Yes			Yes
Aim E Develop study pattern	Yes			
Aim F Understand and make use of peer-group support	Yes	Yes		Yes

Figure 1.1   The matching of study skills to aims

and writing may be broken down further. These groups of skills are reflected in the organization of ideas in this book:

1. Reading skills and the analysis of text:
   (a) reading and note-taking;
   (b) critical analysis of prose and arguments in text (facts and assertions, evidence and sources);
   (c) identifying the key points in a written report;
   (d) dealing with technical material;
   (e) increasing your reading speed.
2. Self-management:
   (a) motivation and learning;
   (b) patterns of concentration and the processing of information;
   (c) time management;
   (d) stress management – the effects of stress, managing yourself, goal-setting, examination preparation.
3. Memory and the organization of information:
   (a) memory;
   (b) diagramming as a means of representing and organizing ideas.
4. Writing and composition:
   (a) outlining and report-writing; planning, writing, revising and finalizing;
   (b) the use of word processors for outlining and composition.

The intention is to introduce you to each of these areas and to improve your study habits and skills. Of course, the improvement can be maintained only if you are prepared to continue to practise the skills by putting them to use. Like the skill of riding a bicycle, learning skills have an element of 'getting the knack of it' in the sense that once learned they are not forgotten, but they do improve with use. Your analysis of your own strengths as a student should help to indicate those skills from which you will benefit most. Conversely you may also discover that some of the techniques taught in this book are just not for you. In a perverse way this is also useful knowledge about yourself which can be put to good effect.

For example, most people find diagramming an invaluable tool for understanding complex problems and for note-taking; for others it seems an unfamiliar technique. But most students quickly discover that diagrams provide a simple and efficient form of shorthand, and an effective way of representing complex ideas which are very difficult to put across in the written word. Even among the 'diagrammers' you will find champions and converts of the different conventions. Later you will be asked to try out all the different techniques and from these select those which suit you best.

You should try to make sure that you include at least one skill for each of the main areas listed above.

Exercise 1.4 contains a short self-test questionnaire on study skills which you can use to set a baseline. This will be the starting point against which you can judge your study skills as they develop. From time to time you may wish to check your progress. The questionnaire is designed so that you can return to it and retest yourself.

NB: Make copies of the blank test first if you wish to re-use the test later.

Exercise 1.4

Some tasks and decisions associated with successful study are set out below.

Assess the difficulty you expect to have in carrying out each task or activity. Then enter on the right a score (1, 2 or 3) for your answer to each question.

If the task or decision:

(a) is a big problem – enter 3;
(b) presents some difficulty – enter 2;
(c) is not a problem for you – enter 1.

How difficult is it for you to . . .

- cope with conflicting priorities: family, work, study, hobbies, etc.?   ——
- choose a suitable place for studying?   ——
- decide when to study or for how long?   ——
- choose study goals?   ——
- decide what to study?   ——
- obtain books and other resources?   ——
- overcome a lack of interest in your own goals?   ——
- deal with activities you dislike?   ——
- cope with doubts about success?   ——
- estimate your own skill level and rate of progress?   ——
- cope with any difficulties in understanding the material?   ——
- concentrate?   ——
- remember facts?   ——
- apply knowledge gained to practice?   ——

- deal with opinions and views instead of facts?   ____
- overcome inertia and laziness?   ____
- share study difficulties with colleagues and
  friends?   ____

Your total score   ====

Now examine your total score. If it is less than 20 you will have few study problems, at least as revealed by this questionnaire, and will find this book a useful refresher course.

If you scored between 20 and 30 you do have some difficulties, and will benefit from spending some time improving your skills.

If you scored 30 or over, probably you are being held back by difficulties with studying. Therefore this course should be of special help to you.

Whatever your present score you should return to this questionnaire from time to time in order to check your progress. Ideally, by the time you have completed the course your score should be less than 20! Try it again as you work through the book and compare your scores.

Remember that this brief questionnaire is not comprehensive. You should interpret your score with care. It gives an indication of the areas in which you may look for improvement.

Managing yourself

The key ingredients in any course are:

1. the study materials;
2. the tutor support (if it is a tutored course); and
3. you and your fellow students.

Only one of these ingredients is under your direct control: you. One of the key aims of this book is to help you to come to terms with your own strengths and weaknesses in study skills and time management.

There will be times when 'giving up' seems too attractive so it is important to establish your own set of objectives for studying. Any adult will have pressures of family, friends and work competing for time. There will be compelling reasons to give more time to work or to your family or to friends – and hence less to study. Any course requires some preparation and dedication. Other work pressures build up and inevitably clash with your study deadlines. Another variation of 'Sodde's law' emerges: if you have a deadline for a study assignment and are falling behind, something urgent will crop up at work or at home!

You will then have to step back and decide if this 'urgent' task is anything more than a 'displacement activity' or way of avoiding a key task. If so, is it giving you another excuse for not keeping to a study plan?

One other way of increasing your commitment to any course is to classify and examine your own particular reasons for starting. Whatever your reasons for embarking on any programme or course, by now you should be able to set them out clearly as a set of objectives. You could group your objectives under two main headings, and consider the following questions:

1. *Job-related training*
   (a) Are there clear professional reasons for studying subject X or Y?
   (b) Do you need a new set of skills in your work?
2. *Personal objectives*
   (a) Will a further qualification enhance your career prospects?
   (b) Are you attracted to the idea of meeting and working alongside a new group of people?

Clear, positive answers to these questions will reinforce your reasons for study. Experience of training courses of many kinds suggests that the strongest motivation comes from your own personal objectives, no matter what advice is given by the boss or training manager.

This section and the previous one have presented a range of study skills. You have assessed your present level of study skills and examined these against your own reasons for undertaking courses to develop further your management skills.

This analysis should now provide the foundation for learning more about individual study skills. In the chapters that follow bear in mind that the analysis is your own assessment of strengths and weaknesses. If you wish, you could consider showing the analysis to a partner or to friends and asking them for their views. Do they think that you have been entirely honest with yourself?

Summary

In this chapter you have been encouraged to examine your working life and career and to consider how study, whether full or part time, might be integrated with other parts of your life.

The motivation and commitment needed for successful study should not be underestimated, but by assessing your strengths in a range of study skills you should be able to identify how best to use the ideas in this book. Ultimately, studying management is much like your job as a manager – it has a lot to do with managing yourself and your time.

2

Study Schedules and Time Management

Overcoming the barriers

There are many difficulties associated with settling down to study. They are well known and experienced by most of us at work and in our private lives. Very few people find it easy to settle to letter writing, serious reading – or even to decorating that room!

This common experience is reassuring. You are not unique if you find that it takes six cups of coffee and a whole packet of biscuits before you can really settle down to work through this text!

Recognizing the existence of barriers and blocks is the first step towards overcoming them. The 'displacement activities' of reading the newspaper, doing housework or making a cup of coffee are ways of getting your mind into gear, though most probably the caffeine over-stimulates you! Many professional authors and novelists freely admit that the displacement activity is inevitable and cannot be eliminated or avoided. They have the confidence to know that afterwards the ideas will flow and the serious writing can begin! Other writers find that stern Victorian self-discipline is needed, and force themselves to sit at their desks and write for a fixed period every day. In your new role as a busy manager and student it may not be so straightforward. You have limited time and limited energy to spend on your new part-time activity. So how can the barriers be overcome?

Goal-setting and rewards

One simple trick is to start with short periods of study, say twenty minutes, and to promise yourself a reward at the end: your favourite television programme, perhaps, a meal, a walk or just a ten-minute break.

Gradually you can extend the study time and change the scale of the reward. Good study habits do not come automatically; the routine must be learned through repetition and practice. But old habits die hard and initially you may find it impossible to avoid collapsing in front of the television every evening. Surveys show that most of the population of the United Kingdom does just this each and every evening! For busy managers this is a serious point, for after a busy and perhaps stressful day or a hectic week in the hurly-burly of a commercial office many feel that they have too little energy to do anything but relax, eat, sleep and do nothing in particular with their limited spare time.

Sharing the problem with your partner can help. Get your husband/wife/partner to set the goal and share the reward. Trivial it may sound, but it is effective. In one household the family agreed that the husband went out with the children every Saturday, leaving the wife at home alone to study on her distance learning course. On returning home they expected a progress report, not excuses and certainly not supper cooked by the 'student'!

Learning patterns and preferences

One of the important skills involved in becoming an effective learner is the ability to step back and examine your progress and use of time. The ideas behind 'work study' are not new nor need they be particularly sophisticated. Most work routines in factories and offices have been analysed and improved by changing the order in which individual operations are performed or by modifying the layout. Even a modern kitchen can be laid out to minimize the distance covered in the most frequent journeys: between refrigerator, work surface and cooker, and between cooker and sink.

Your study patterns need be no different. In the next section we will examine how you use time at present and create a plan or strategy for managing your use of time during the period of any course you undertake. It will not be perfect nor will you be able to maintain your studies unerringly, but a framework for study will enable you to give time to your course and to your other commitments.

Analysing your use of time

The first requirement if you are about to embark on a course lasting some months or a year or more is to analyse your use of time. Since we are not assuming a time and motion study in which you are followed by someone with a stop-watch and clipboard you will have to estimate for yourself how you use time over a suitable period of one or two days.

For this a desk diary or notebook will be adequate. Imagine you charge for your time by the half-hour. This is not unusual: in many fields, such as law and accountancy, it is common for firms to expect that their professional staff will be able to attribute up to 60 per cent of the working time directly to clients.

The purpose of the exercise is not to discover if you are working efficiently but rather to seek out some 'dead' time in your working day. Are you an early riser with time to spare in the morning? Do you have a long commuting journey which could be used for study? Could you rearrange your leisure activities to create a free evening or dedicate alternate weekends to study?

Exercise 2.1

Do not spend more than an hour on this exercise in total.

Select two different days, e.g. a working day and a weekend day, from a one-week period and record your use of time at approximately thirty-minute intervals from the time you wake to the time you go to sleep. Use the chart provided to record your use of time. Alternatively, you could use a diary or even a spreadsheet on a personal computer.

You should now try to produce a revised plan for your use of time while studying in the future.

This detailed level of analysis is needed because we are trying to identify short periods of 'dead' time which could be used more effectively or, brought together, could give you opportunities for study. You will need to be clear in your mind whether an activity is 'play' or 'work', and whether or not 'pottering about' is really necessary.

Day One	Activity	Possible study time?
0700		
0730		
0800		
0830		
0900		
0930		
1000		
1030		
1100		
1130		
1200		
1230		
1300		
1330		
1400		
1430		
1500		
1530		
1600		
1630		
1700		
1730		
1800		
1830		
1900		
1930		
2000		
2030		
2100		
2130		
2200		
2230		
2300		
2330		
2400		

Estimated time available for study _____

Examine the record and then group the time usage into appropriate categories, e.g. work, leisure, sport, eating, housework, travel, etc. Your pattern may vary from week to week in which case you will have to adjust the recording period or choose an 'average' week.

Try to identify crisis patterns and to assess the impact of urgent meetings, etc. on your schedule. Do you build in time to allow for these contingencies?

Finally, add up the 'dead' time or time which could be used for other or dual uses. (Can you read while on the train? Do the ironing while watching television? Study during the lunch break at work?)

Compare this figure with the weekly study time for your course. If you are very lucky your employer may even have allocated study time during the working week, but in the United Kingdom this is still rare for middle and senior managers. For most part-time study you should be looking for between ten and twenty hours per week. Whatever the 'design' time of the course a 30 per cent increase will allow you some flexibility and opportunity for extra reading around the subject area of your course.

You may wish to make extra copies of the blank chart before you start. You can then use them to record other days and any revised plans you may formulate.

Setting up your study schedule

Knowing how much time could be given over to study is only part of the answer. Experience from project planning and scheduling tells us that some 'redundancy' is needed to cope with contingencies of ordinary life. For example, the schedule for any construction project will allow some time for bad weather and delays in the delivery of materials. So with any study plan you should build in some slack time for the unexpected work assignment, trip or period of illness.

Use the information from Exercise 2.1 to develop a provisional weekly study plan, and then get someone else to look at it. Invariably the objective view of a third party will reveal some over-optimism. Ask your partner to see if the pattern is realistic for the whole of the period of the course. Have you allowed for holidays, etc.? Your partner can also help by monitoring your study routine and by applying a little judicious pressure to make sure that you stick to it.

Use the blank timetable form in Table 2.1 to draw up a rough study plan and, as before, make some copies before you start so that

Table 2.1   An outline study plan

Day	a.m.	p.m.	Evening
Monday			
Tuesday			
Wednesday			
Thursday			
Friday			
Saturday			
Sunday			

you can revise and update your schedule until you arrive at a realistic and workable strategy.

Such a plan may seem trivial and not worth the work involved in generating it, but setting a pattern, sharing it and then keeping to it are not trivial tasks. You may well find that you have to start with quite modest goals and then work up to your full plan as the study habit is developed. If you decide to make a long-term commitment to a programme of study, the study plan and a fairly steady routine will be essential.

The limitations of any schedule

Almost any schedule will have flaws and require modification. You will need to review your study plan after a few weeks and redefine how to use your time.

There will also be occasions on a long course when the plan breaks down completely. Re-establishing it will then be a priority if progress is to be maintained. You may also discover that plans simply don't fit your personality and lifestyle: knowing and understanding this can be useful. If you have no pattern of leisure, study and work and you feel that your life is pressured and chaotic, it may well be that for you study and work are incompatible. You may then reach the conclusion that the study will have to be ditched. If you do this, at least you will have the satisfaction of understanding why, and not simply be left with feelings of 'not coping'. A new task will be clear – that of getting your life back under your own control!

The time-planning exercise above assumes that a regular pattern of study can be achieved and that it suits the majority of managers. However, if you do not fit this pattern you will have to develop an alternative plan and set aside periods for intensive study. One manager with a demanding workload and a busy family life found that the best way to study and to keep up with her open learning course was to take two or three days' leave at intervals. This solution eliminated any plans for a long summer break but it did ensure uninterrupted periods of intensive study.

Organizations are now giving better support to employees on part-time and open learning courses and it is not uncommon for staff to be given time out for study on approved courses.

Keeping track of your own progress can be difficult as many courses draw on a range of books and manuals. For some students and adult learners a notebook has proved useful as a study diary and as a means of keeping a check on progress. The specialized planners and organizers, such as the Filofax, come into their own for this purpose. You should certainly consider the idea of a special notebook or diary. Would it suit you? Will it fit your briefcase? Is it a convenient size for note-taking? The notebook can go everywhere with you and be used for jottings on articles you read, talks you hear and plans for assignments, reports, etc. It can then form the basis of revision notes and provide you with a purpose-made guide to your selected course. Your own notes can in this way gradually replace the course materials.

The best first – and last – resort if you get into difficulties with your studies is, of course, the help of another person. The earlier discussion about help has implied that this should come from a member of your family but there may well be individuals in your company who have experience of part-time study. If so seek them out and share the difficulties with them – but remember that time-management is only one aspect of successful study.

People do differ widely in their ability to plan and use time; the important task is to find a method or strategy which fits your lifestyle and suits you.

The study environment

The choice of a place to study in comfort and in peace and quiet is important. But with a little planning you will be able to study and work effectively in crowded and noisy offices, in trains and on planes. However, for most of us peace and quiet are desirable if we are to concentrate effectively, and this is particularly true for writing and serious reading.

Of somewhat lesser importance is the question of space for working, storage for books and papers, and access to reference materials. If you are in the fortunate position of having a study or den of your own at home this section may not be for you, but in the discussion below we will consider a number of other options which can increase the flexibility of your study sessions.

The ideal workplace is undoubtedly a private study with good lighting, ample shelving, a large table or desk, a good desk-chair and a comfortable armchair. For many people the best compromise is a spare bedroom. This will at least allow you to organize your books and papers and to leave them prepared and undisturbed. *And you, and you alone, should do the dusting and cleaning.* Asking someone else in your household to help is only asking for trouble. If you do it yourself, it's clearly *your* fault when papers go missing, and you will have removed one source of friction in the student household.

The shared use of rooms is more difficult. Your times for using the room must be negotiated, and you must remember to allow for the time to set out your papers and to file them away at the end of each session. But in every household something can be done to give a student a study corner of some kind.

A kitchen or dining table will usually be big enough to allow you to spread out work papers and books, and you might be able to persuade the rest of your household to leave you in peace for a couple of hours after supper during the week. Alternatively, banish the family or adopt a late night/early morning study habit.

One doctor who returned to study in his late thirties found another solution. Joining his children for an organized session of homework from Monday to Thursday was an ideal way of creating a regular study pattern and ensuring peace and quiet – with benefits for the rest of the family as well.

For most people it is important at times to get away from the home to study. Most public libraries have reading rooms which are open in the evening, some even have private study booths or carrels – another way of securing that all-important peace and quiet. You may also find that the act of going out to the library is just the right preliminary task to put you in the mood for study. The only drawback is the pressure on space in many public library reading rooms, especially at GCSE exam times when all the teenagers in your neighbourhood will take over every available corner!

Storage of books and papers

As in any office it is important to keep your books and papers well organized. Any shared or intermittent use of a desk or table will mean that you will need storage for books and materials. You may find that a shelf is adequate for textbooks and bound material, but box files, plastic storage boxes or ring-binders are needed to keep under control all the other paperwork associated with any course. Even humble cardboard boxes can provide the answer. They are free and can easily be cut down to fit A4 files and papers. Students with the Open University often claim that sorting, filing and managing the administrative paperwork is the hardest part of their studies!

On the move

If you travel a great deal a better solution may be to use a separate case for your study materials. It keeps the books separate from work papers, and opening the study case can be your own cue for mentally switching off from everyday concerns and turning to your studies. It may even be sufficient to ensure that the current assignment or piece of reading is always handy in your briefcase or bag. The traveller or commuter has many opportunities to fit in study. Delayed trains and planes force you to wait, so why not use the time productively?

Train and plane journeys do not necessarily mean dead time. Reading and note-taking can easily be done while travelling in this way, even in relatively short and intermittent bursts of ten to twenty minutes. Report-writing on the move is the one study activity that does not work. By all means make your notes and plan an essay, but leave the actual writing and composition until you are at your desk, unless you are fortunate enough to have a lap-top personal computer.

The motorist faces more difficulties. Some courses make limited use of audiotapes and you may be able to listen to these in the car. Be prepared to listen to each track several times over a period of days, and you will find that a good understanding and knowledge of the material can be gained in this way. If the tape is of the 'stop the tape now' variety listening on the move is ruled out. For this you will need the peace and quiet of your study.

If your work requires you to travel a great deal remember that hotel rooms make ideal private studies. A modest degree of ingenuity and some pre-planning can turn a trip away from home into a valuable period of course work. Decide how you will use the time available and take the necessary materials with you.

Learning in groups

So far the discussion about the learning environment has assumed that you are working alone and independently for much of the time. However, if the course is run for your organization you may find that tutorials are arranged at your place of work, or that you can find time for lunchtime 'work-ins' with colleagues. If this is so it will pay to create a good setting for team or group work.

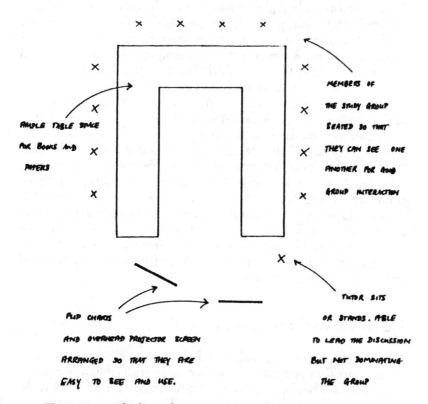

Figure 2.1   The horseshoe arrangement for good group work

Avoid having a classroom set up. In general try to arrange to work in groups of seven or less and to sit in a semi-circle where you can all watch one another while listening. Tables are unnecessary unless some particular activity requires them. Notes can be made on a pad and there are real benefits to be gained from having space in which to move around. Some psychologists would even claim that the way in which any discussion moves forward is influenced by the physical arrangement of the room, and that 'body-language' provides clues and cues to which we all respond subconsciously. With the chairs arranged in a circle or horseshoe and any table removed, individuals are more open and relaxed and listen to one another more carefully. Figure 2.1 illustrates this arrangement.

You may be assuming that this advice applies only to tutors. It doesn't. The responsibility for creating a good setting for group interaction and participation rests with both student and tutor.

Small-group work can be very enjoyable, but it should also be creative and stimulating. As a student you should not tolerate badly designed study settings or badly run sessions in which you are expected only to sit and listen. In management education as in most fields, active involvement generates learning and a well-designed setting can enhance this. A badly designed physical setting for group work is inhibiting and stressful.

Rearrange the furniture at the start of a session. It breaks the ice and creates a good atmosphere if several of you share the task. Many advocates of small-group discussion also encourage the use of flipcharts for recording ideas and key points as a way of enhancing learning. If you have the opportunity to use these remember that they provide a focus for discussion, enable the group to develop a shared summary of any topic and generate a sense of involvement as students take turns in recording ideas or producing diagrams. In group work have different people lead the discussion, and change the leadership every twenty minutes or so. That way everybody stays lively and attentive to the debate, with the flipchart or white-board providing a focal point of interest.

Libraries and reference sources

Anyone returning to learning will discover sooner or later that it is essential to find and use a good library to track down important references and books. Nowadays many courses are designed to be self-contained and all the books and other materials are provided.

Even so, if you want to avoid the cost of buying additional books the regular use of a good library is vital for any wider reading.

It will make you a better student if you read around the course. Many companies have their own reference library stocking the relevant management and technical journals to which you may need access. Otherwise you will need to use the local library.

Choosing a self-contained courses is clearly a wise choice to begin with, but if you do decide to enrol for any course with a project or research element you will need to use libraries. You should then consider using computer literature searches and microfiche readers. Most libraries charge for computer searches, but they can save time and help you to track down specialist materials.

The 'serious' daily and weekly newspapers are an excellent source of topical information. Many have weekly features on a range of industrial and management topics. In addition, there may well be relevant trade journals and magazines to follow up and read.

Self-help groups, peer-group support and co-counselling

Many managers on training courses say that they learn more from other managers than from the instructors. If this is so and you are isolated from other students, any residential seminars or short courses will be especially important. It does seem that the process of learning, clarifying and understanding is best done by discussion within a small group and not by the individual studying in isolation. In this sense management development is both an intellectual *and* a social process. Many of the part-time degrees run by business schools have regular residential weekend schools, enabling the participants to come together for team and group work and to take part in special sessions. Events of this kind allow for a great deal of informal interaction and provide an ideal opportunity for reviewing progress with other members of your peer group and for comparing methods of study.

Clearly, discussion within your study group and with your colleagues is essential. Team working is a way of checking your understanding in a non-threatening environment. Colleagues at work can be sympathetic, helpful and effective as a sounding board for new ideas with which you are experimenting. Any management course will suggest ideas and techniques which you will want to apply in practice. You will need to explain what you are doing and why, and to discuss any new proposals thoroughly.

The overall message of this section is that you can improve your study skills by working with others. Study is frequently seen to be a lonely, introspective activity, and can be stressful particularly when undertaken in addition to the normal responsibilities and demands of a full-time job. Working with others can reduce stress simply by allowing you and your colleagues to share any problems associated with the course being undertaken. If you find a congenial colleague who is also taking your course, so much the better. You can work on a one-to-one basis and help each other with your studies. For many people this sort of simple co-counselling, or 'buddy system', can work well.

You could both set targets and goals for study activities and then compare progress after a fixed period of time, say a week. Your discussion could then proceed with an analysis of any impediments to study. In this way you will be able to understand the causes of any overload and to identify ways of overcoming particular study difficulties.

If you decide to try this, remember the following key points.

1. Set aside time for regular meetings with a colleague to review your progress. Stick to the agreement.
2. Plan your sessions so that you cannot be interrupted.
3. Divide the time equally between talking and listening.
4. Set individual study goals and compare your progress with that of your colleague.
5. Try to view your study goals as a 'learning contract'.

Summary

This chapter has addressed the ever-present issue of how to make best use of your time. Studying how you use time now is the start of learning how you might make changes to free more time for your new study tasks. Setting sensible goals is one part of this, understanding when and how you can work most effectively is another. Allowing time for family and leisure activities is just as important in the longer term as study and work so these must not be forgotten.

Group study and the use of time in such settings are as important as your use of private study time. Methods to improve the effectiveness of work done with your colleagues will yield dividends; not only will you find that you learn more, but through contributing more you should find that group work can be most enjoyable as well as effective.

3
Information:
Coping with It All

In this chapter we will examine the ideas of information and memory and their implications for the process of learning.

Information and theories about information were very topical in the 1980s, the age of 'information technology', but here we are concerned only with information in the general sense of visual and aural stimulation of the brain. How do we receive, transmit and encode information? How does memory work?

The purpose here is to help you to understand enough about memory, the mind and the way in which we process information to decide how you might best attack the tasks of learning and memory which are associated with study.

The message is in essence very simple. The human brain is an extremely complex and efficient system for managing our physiological well-being. In normal everyday activities we use only a relatively small part of the capacity of the brain for thinking and processing 'information'. So whatever else we may have been told at school, we are all able to make use of and take advantage of the brain's immense capabilities.

Receiving information

In simple terms we receive information continually through the senses of smell, taste, sight, hearing and touch. Our ability to integrate and make sense of the continuous stream of stimuli turns data (the individual stimuli) into information. The brain and

nervous system are extremely complex and even today our knowledge of how information is stored and encoded is limited. Many
theories of memory and learning exist in competition with one
another. So it is not possible to give simple, clear-cut answers to any
questions about the size of our brain and the way in which it
functions.

Although our knowledge of the brain is far from complete we do
know that it is much more subtle and complex than previously
thought. There are some useful explanatory models of the brain on
which we can draw to understand something of the principles of
memory and creative thinking.

How your mind works

One of the most useful models of brain function is based on our
knowledge of the different roles played by the right and left halves
of the brain. Much of our knowledge has come from studies of the
impairment of brain function such as that suffered by the victims of
certain illnesses and physical injuries. At its simplest we now
understand that each side of the brain controls different functions.
Thus the left hemisphere controls the right side of the body and the
right brain the left side of the body. This gives rise to the 'right-brain,
left-brain' model, as exemplified by Figure 3.1.

This simple model can help us to understand some important
features of the learning process. For example, creativity and intuition
are associated with the right brain (or more accurately with the
cerebral cortex), and logical reasoning and analysis with the left
brain or cerebral cortex. At its extreme you may encounter the
inappropriate use of this terminology. Artistic or musical people are
sometimes described as 'right brain people' and those with a flair for
mathematics and reasoning 'left brain' people. Such labels are
misleading for not only do we all use both hemispheres but there are
many interconnections.

One of the contradictions of neurophysiology is that every
discovery seems only to reveal yet more complexity in the brain. This
would appear to imply that improving your 'brain' skills is equally
complex. Fortunately it's not so and a range of simple tools and
techniques based on a simple model of brain function can enable you
to increase your mental performance.

Of course the 'right-brain, left-brain' model is oversimplified. As
has been suggested, both sides work with each other and are
interconnected, although in behavioural terms it is common for

THE 'DIVISION' OF THE CEREBRAL CORTEX

INTO TWO PARTS GIVES RISE TO THE IDEAS

OF THE RIGHT BRAIN AND THE LEFT BRAIN.

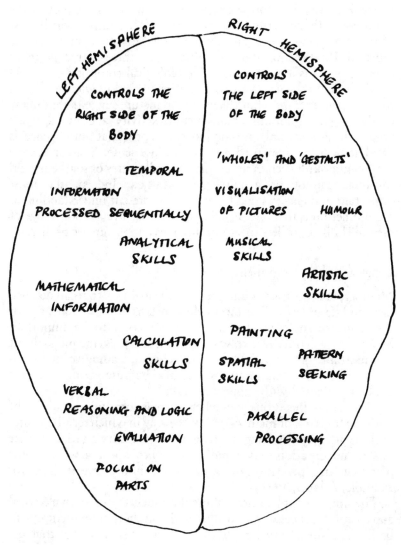

Figure 3.1   The right-brain, left-brain model

individuals to display traits indicating dominance of one side or other. Even the most sophisticated models of brain function are inadequate explanations of an extremely complex biological process. For example, in attempts to measure or estimate the brain's complexity it is usual to use the number of cells or the interconnections between them. But there are not enough noughts to describe the number: more interconnections than there are atoms in the universe is one estimate! The cortex or grey matter which is the part of the brain associated with thinking and learning is the part to which most of this discussion refers. This deeply folded mantle contains in the order of 100,000 million cells alone! The three-pound brain of *Homo sapiens* is a quite remarkable biological computer.

All the natural sciences are contributing to our knowledge of brain function and memory, but the emerging picture suggests that many of the accepted notions about mental activity and memory are untenable. For example, it is no longer accepted that 'intelligence' is fixed and can be 'measured' in any absolute sense. Nor can we say that mental skills such as the ability to recall poetry or mathematical formulae cannot be acquired and learned. Indeed, the most important and encouraging feature of our present understanding of brain function is that we can enhance and improve a whole range of mental skills regardless of age or any ideas about innate ability.

Long- and short-term memory

Memory, or more usually and precisely the inability to recall detailed facts and figures at will, is one of the concerns of most students. For the management student recall may not seem to be important because the job usually involves reasoning and judgemental skills. It *is* important, however, because most courses leading to qualifications still involve examinations, and also because good arguments are best presented with supporting data.

Fortunately this is one area where there is some understanding of both the function of memory and of the way in which recall operates in the typical study setting when an individual is trying to assimilate lots of information very rapidly. It is also an area where some planning and practice can bring about improvement (see, for example, Adams, 1988).

The simplest explanations of memory suggest that both electrical and chemical processes are involved and that short-term memory can be distinguished from long-term memory. It is suggested that the process of short-term memory operates through information being

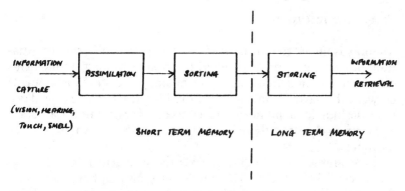

Figure 3.2   Short and long term memory: an information processing
model

encoded and stored as electrical activity in the brain. At this level the
model of the brain as a computer is appealing and is still seen by
many as a good representation of brain function. Signals are received
by the eye, ear and other senses and transmitted to the brain as
electrical impulses in nerves. In the brain itself it is suggested that
data are held as patterns of electrical charge in the manner of a
computer memory.

However, long-term memory is thought to be different: it is
suggested that it works by converting information through chemical
processes in which the different patterns of electrical activity in the
brain during sleep play a part.

Thus these processes of long- and short-term memory are linked
to the contrasting patterns of electrical activity in the brain which
occur during sleep and periods of alertness. For example, it is
suggested the 'cramming' for exam revision may work because
information which is stored in short-term memory in some form of
electrical activity is converted into long-term or 'chemical' memory
during the period of sleep which follows. The successful student then
finds that the information can be recalled efficiently the following
day.

Sleep and study habits, and in particular the use of reading
techniques during study, have an important role in memory. It
follows that your own study pattern should be designed to take
account of this, ensuring that you have the opportunity to
concentrate on your studies and yet also have enough relaxation,
exercise and sleep.

Processing information

Memory is linked to information processing, but the term 'information' has meaning only through association or context. In the fields of computing and information technology a distinction is made between the terms 'data' and 'information'. Data can be considered to be the individual numbers and letters or words, while information is the arrangement of those numbers and words in a way which has meaning.

For example, as an English-speaker the arrangement of data, e.g. the letters E-N-G-L-A-N-D, conveys information, but to the non-English-speaker familiar with our alphabet it is only a string of letters with no special meaning, i.e. data. For a Russian, Greek, Chinese or Japanese reader the letters are merely a set of symbols which bear no apparent relation to their own languages.

The term 'information processing' implies that data are being organized so that they have meaning to the recipient. In reading or listening this is precisely the kind of processing which is going on. In the mind the data are being organized into patterns which carry meaning and information.

The preparation of notes, writing, speech, and the act of drawing up a diagram are all examples of information being processed and encoded. Less obvious are the processes of thought and memory which take place at a subconscious level.

In the story of Archimedes leaping from his bath in ancient Greece shouting 'Eureka!' we appear to have an example of information processing at the subconscious level. The flash of inspiration as he finally solved the puzzle of density and volumetric measurement by displacement seems to have occurred as he relaxed. The act of making sense of the observation which led to the subsequent development of the theory of displacement as a measure of volume appears to have been triggered at this moment of relaxation. We do process information efficiently, but on occasion this happens indirectly. Most of us are familiar with the problem of being unable to recall a name or face only to find it springing to mind later when we have turned our attention to some other task. This phenomenon is probably also linked to operations of the subconscious mind as described above.

The phrase 'sleep on it' appears to be extremely good advice if we take account of our understanding of brain function. Sleep not only allows us to rest physically but also apparently allows us to sort and organize information.

Using memory techniques

It is commonly assumed by adult students that they will be unable to recall information simply because they are 'not young any more'. While there is some correlation between age and memory it should not deter us from undertaking study or from using techniques which can help us to recall new and unfamiliar ideas.

In Chapter 4 you will find that diagrams are suggested as a powerful tool for helping us to organize and recall ideas, but in addition you can use other techniques to help with the assimilation, retention and recall of information.

The association of ideas is perhaps the most commonly used device. By searching for a connecting theme between ideas we can generate a 'thread' of reasoning which will lead from one idea to another as we start the process of recall. Many memory games depend on our ability to recall an image of the arrangement of objects and to visualize and thus recall the absent items. This also appears to work because of the connections between objects which

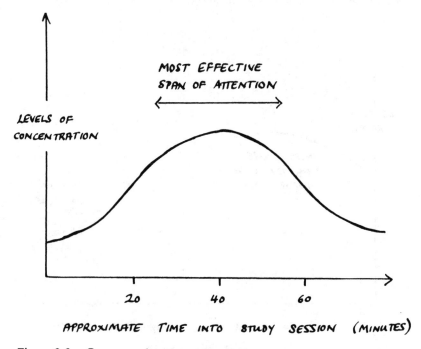

Figure 3.3   Concentration patterns over time

then yield a pattern. Mnemonics and word-association as memory aids appear to work in the same fashion. This ability to recall names and lists can be learned and enhanced. You can even devise simple tests to measure your improvements.

There is a link between study time, concentration and recall which is revealed if we look at a typical graph of concentration patterns over time in a typical one-hour lecture, as shown in Figure 3.3. The figure shows a build up, a twenty-minute period of peak effectiveness and then a period of declining attention. For the lecturer or speaker this has implications for the organization of the ideas to be put across. Clearly the key concepts should be put into the central twenty-minute period. For the student the lessons are equally plain: in an ideal study period there will be a warm-up phase, a period of peak effectiveness and then a decline.

These ideas also give us some suggestions for the design of private study sessions. Planned sessions should not be overlong, should contain some short breaks and the most demanding or serious work should be placed at the centre of any one-hour study period.

Figure 3.4 tells us that the ability to recall information after a period of study rises for a while and then decays gradually over time.

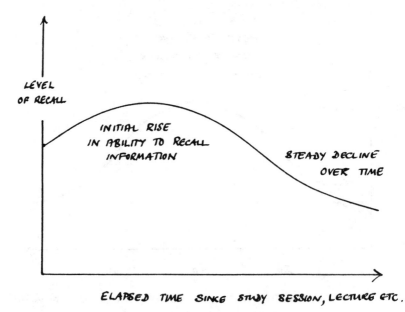

Figure 3.4   The decline in recall over time

This supports the argument that important processing of information takes place *after* the study period, so it is clearly important to allow time for this to occur – by relaxing or even perhaps revising or writing up notes for a little while after a formal study period.

Other studies of university students in Australia support this conclusion (Maddox, 1988). Students who regularly revised and updated their lecture notes at the end of each day consistently performed better. The recall and organization process was being helped along. Whatever study pattern you choose to adopt the evidence points to some advantages from regular study and periods of revision.

Your 'filing' system

The storage of information is another confusing area for the psychologists and biologists, and cannot easily be separated from the question of recall.

It can be argued that all the steps we take to improve reading speed and note-taking skills are in fact actions which improve the organization of information prior to storage. 'Assimilation' is the term used to describe this organizing activity which links the eye and hand movements of reading and writing to the storage of information in the mind. Complex interactions are taking place and it is too simple to think of the process as a simple one-way transfer of information to the brain.

A better image of this process is that of information being organized and stored ready for 'filing away'. Then, later, during sleep and relaxation the job of 'filing 'is actually done. Even this oversimplifies the process for it still does not include an explanation of the further subconscious organization of the information which is taking place. Later, in Chapter 5 we look further at ways of improving reading skills.

Listening and learning

The task of listening is not often considered demanding or worthy of attention. Yet we all know that in a long and interesting meeting just listening attentively and thinking through arguments as they are presented can be demanding and exhausting. You can improve your listening skills through active listening: watching the speaker carefully and by having a plan or method of note-taking. When the opportunity next arises try to watch a speaker carefully. You should find that you listen better as well.

In the next chapter several diagramming techniques are introduced. One or other of these may suit you as a form of shorthand for note-taking.

The lecture or tutorial is a one-to-many setting in which you will be one of the 'many' in your new role as student. It is perhaps a little difficult to think of listening 'actively' in that setting. You can overcome this by treating the lecture as if it were a one-to-one session. Watch the speaker and concentrate on the task of listening. In one-to-one interviews this is even more important. Your behaviour as a listener can influence the discussion. Open questions can encourage longer and more revealing answers. An abrupt question or interruption can force the speaker to 'close up'. Interviewing skills are beyond the scope of this book, but in management development they are an important skill which is closely allied to the learning skills taught here.

Listening is one skill area where you can improve day by day. Make use of every opportunity at work, in meetings and in conferences to learn to listen 'actively'. You will be pleasantly surprised at the outcome. Listening is of course not just a study skill, it is also an important management skill. In all settings it is not only what is said that is important, but what is *not* said and how information is conveyed. The term 'body language' is used to describe the subconscious actions which betray our emotions, but it is also important that you respond appropriately to the tone of the speaker's voice. As a manager in your one-to-one dealings with people you will already be aware of the importance of mood and tone. In the training setting this is perhaps less so for it is the information content which is most important, but even in such settings mood and tone convey the nuances of meaning.

In your management studies, indeed in your role as a manager, the need for these skills is not restricted to the tutorial setting. Later if you decide to opt for a project-based course you will almost certainly find yourself needing interviewing skills which include not only the ability to phrase questions appropriately but also the ability to listen 'actively'.

Summary

In this chapter we have moved at high speed through a vast area of research and knowledge concerning brain function, memory and recall. Clearly it is a superficial treatment of an important topic, but for us there are some key points to bear in mind.

1. Both creative and analytical skills can be used effectively in organizing and carrying through your studies.
2. Understanding the idea of long- and short-term memory should allow you to plan your use of study time, so that when necessary you can improve your ability to recall information at will.
3. In lectures and tutorials try to make notes in a structured fashion and to listen 'actively'.

4

Diagrams as an Aid to Thinking and Learning

'A diagram is worth a thousand words' is the claim. In the exercises of this chapter you should discover whether this is so for you. Undoubtedly diagrams as a means of representing and recalling knowledge work better for some than for others. But if you can make them work you will have acquired a powerful tool for learning and communication. A modest degree of skill will enable you to produce satisfying images and, fortunately, the conventions of some of the commonly used techniques are simple, easy to follow and can be practised by merely 'doodling'.

In the discussion which follows four diagramming techniques will be introduced. The different forms can be used as tools to help in the following tasks:

1. note-taking while listening;
2. note-taking while reading;
3. outlining and report planning;
4. thinking through complex problems;
5. developing shared representations of problems in group work;
6. summarizing situations;
7. exploring the dynamics of organizational change;
8. exploring the structure of situations.

You may now be wondering why diagrams are better than the written word. The answer lies in the mechanisms of the brain and the problems posed by the structure of text. Text has to be a linear string of words and symbols, and the spoken word is restricted in a similar way. Studies of art and painting suggest that there are important relationships between the spatial arrangement of images in a picture and the way in which an observer's eye tracks or travels around the different parts of the composition. Thus 'good' representational art has a balance and is able to evoke strong feelings from us. We can view diagrams in a similar fashion. A well-prepared diagram gives an instant image of a 'whole' and its internal organization is able to show the relationship between the component parts. The diagram is also liberating in the sense that it is not bound by the limits of grammar or vocabulary. Many people find that after a short period of practice the diagram becomes an indispensable aid to planning written reports and presentations. Being able to put the 'whole' plan on a single piece of paper and to organize a set of ideas is appealing.

Some psychologists explain artistic and diagramming skills in terms of the contrast between logical reasoning and creativity, which was discussed earlier. The right brain and left brain appear to be centres which have special roles. Creativity and artistic skill are usually associated with right-brain activity. One of the best-known diagramming conventions for note-taking is the 'mind map'.

Figure 4.2 is an example of a mind map. It uses the technique to explore the ideas associated with learning in this book. The branches show linked sets of ideas, and the arrows show how later I was able look at some possible interactions and interconnections. A revision of the figure might show those branches linked by arrows in a different position to bring these particular ideas closer together.

The psychologist Tony Buzan (1974) based this diagram on a model of brain and memory. Buzan appears to be supporting the claim that information in the brain is not processed serially (that is, as a string of data handled piece by piece), but in chunks or wholes which are managed in parallel. This suggests that learning can be improved when the input of information takes this form. The theory supports the use of diagrams to present information in this 'chunky' form.

The model of the brain as a machine like a digital computer which processes information in a serial manner is now less well supported. It is being replaced by a model based on the current developments in computing, artificial intelligence and expert systems, which are increasingly taking advantage of electronic devices capable of parallel processing. This work in its turn seems to match our more sophisticated contemporary model of brain function. Ideas about computing and brain function thus seem to remain in step as our knowledge improves.

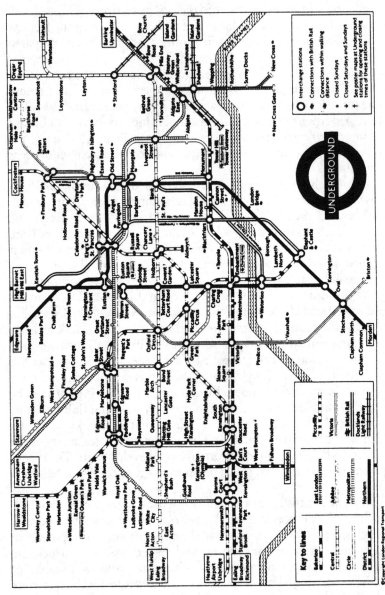

Figure 4.1   The London Underground system

Similarly, when we look at the way people learn and absorb ideas we find that those analytical approaches which emphasize parts are giving way to synthetic or holistic approaches which instead look more and more for the links or relationships which make up a whole. In schools the curriculum no longer simply divides knowledge into watertight compartments, but instead brings different skills to bear on topics and problems which cross the old boundaries. Many of the criticisms of the recent reforms of education were based on fears that they will reverse this trend towards an integrated curriculum. Management education has some similar characteristics in so far as it brings together skills and techniques which can be used in a practical fashion in the workplace.

One celebrated diagram which simplifies and clarifies a complex setting is the map of the London Underground (see Figure 4.1). The system's general features and organization are clearly shown in two dimensions, giving us some good hints for successful diagramming. The careful arrangement of the lines and the choice of colours have the effect of simplifying the network. Much of the detail is redundant and is not included: the many bends and twists are not shown, neither is the depth below street level of the individual lines – you do not need this information to use the map so it is not included. Scale is represented only in a crude sense but even so the essential information on the sequence of stations, the points where it is possible to transfer to other lines, and the relative positions of the various lines is accurate. Early versions of the map were in black and white with colour being added as the lines grew in number. Good diagrams should be simple, clear and easy to follow.

Mind mapping and other diagrams

The term 'mind map' as coined by Buzan (1974) describes a form of diagram which he found to be a valuable tool for sorting, organizing and presenting ideas. His work with children and students showed that the technique was simple and easy to use and could be learned very quickly. Its advantages are the same as those of any good diagrammimg convention; namely that it should be easily under-stood and that it is easy for a novice to master. Figure 4.2 describes the contents of this book and shows how several pages of text can be replaced by a suitable diagram.

Figure 4.3 shows the 'mind map' convention as it might be used to explain the uses and properties of a number of different kinds of

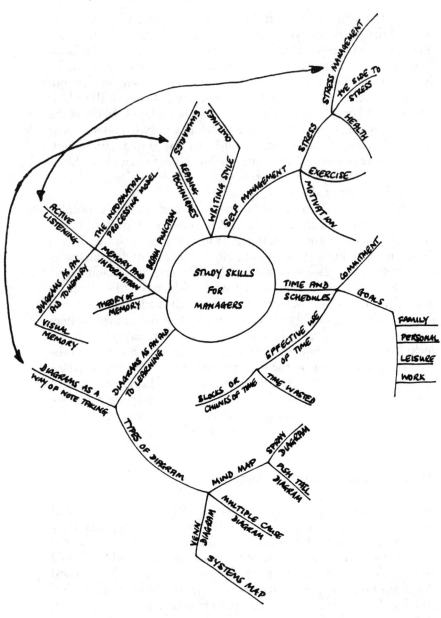

Figure 4.2   A mind map of *Study Skills for Managers*

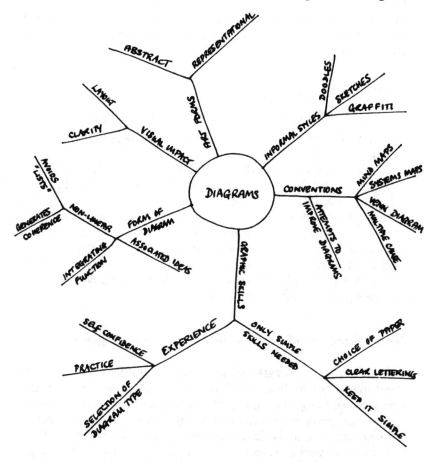

Figure 4.3   A mind map to show some of the properties of different
types of diagrams

diagram. Examine it carefully, and you will see that there are many
different uses and conventions for diagrams apart from those which
we will examine in this course.

An A4 page gives adequate space for setting out most diagrams
but its small size means that it is unsuitable if more than one person
wants to contribute to the development of a diagram. Flipcharts and
white-boards are now familiar objects in the offices and conference
rooms of many organizations and provide ideal surfaces for
diagrammers. Their large size allows flipcharts, etc. to be used by a
group, and coloured pens enable you to highlight different features

and sets of ideas. Rolls of lining paper and sheets of Contiboard provide a cheaper domestic alternative to the somewhat expensive office items.

Exercise 4.1

Do not spend more than fifteen minutes on this exercise.

1. Use the mind-map technique to describe your job and responsibilities.

   Then show the result to a friend or colleague who is unfamiliar with the details of your work and ask him or her to use it to give you an account of your job.

   You should be surprised. In most cases this exercise enables other people to produce impressive descriptions of one's own job and organization from nothing more than a single diagram.
2. Imagine you are asked to produce a job description for a new staff member. Spend a few minutes planning the description using the mind-map technique.

Note-taking: mind maps, fish-tail and spray diagrams

Fish-tail and spray diagrams can be seen as simple variants of the mind-map diagram. Fish-tail diagrams were developed in Japan as a device for thinking through questions of quality control – another area of management where success depends on an appreciation of the links between the individual stages of a process or operation. They can also be viewed as a single part of a mind map. Figure 4.4 shows this simple convention and the spray diagram, which uses a single fixed convention of lines on which labels are written. This contrasts with the mind map, which is more variable with curves and circles as well as labelled lines. Try out the conventions and choose the one that suits you best.

Thinking in structures: Venn diagrams and systems maps

In contrast to the previous diagrams, which are used mainly to explore ideas, you will also have occasion when a diagram may be needed to understand the structure of an organization or firm. The Venn diagram is used in schools to teach children about sets or entities which have common properties. In the formal Venn diagram

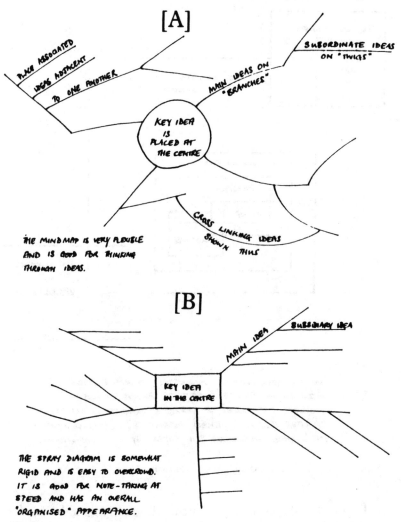

[A]

PLACE ASSOCIATED IDEAS ADJACENT TO ONE ANOTHER

MAIN IDEAS ON "BRANCHES"

SUBORDINATE IDEAS ON "TWIGS"

KEY IDEA IS PLACED AT THE CENTRE

THE MIND MAP IS VERY FLEXIBLE AND IS GOOD FOR THINKING THROUGH IDEAS.

CROSS LINKING IDEAS SHOWN THUS

[B]

MAIN IDEA

SUBSIDIARY IDEA

KEY IDEA IN THE CENTRE

THE SPRAY DIAGRAM IS SOMEWHAT RIGID AND IS EASY TO OVERCROWD. IT IS GOOD FOR NOTE-TAKING AT SPEED AND HAS AN OVERALL "ORGANISED" APPEARANCE.

Figure 4.4   Diagrams: two of a kind   A. The mind map
B. The spray diagram

convention boxes and rectangles are nested within one another or overlaid to show the common membership by components of different sets. This form of representation is useful for structures when you are sure about the arrangement, as in, say, the case of the structure of your company.

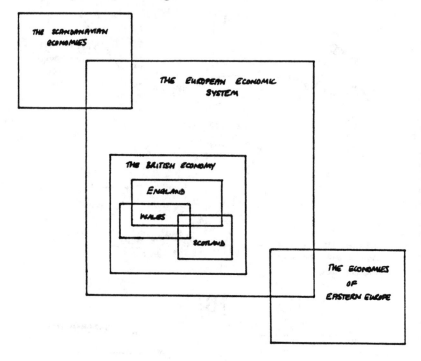

IN THE VENN DIAGRAM CONVENTION COMMON ENTITIES ARE
INCLUDED IN THE SAME SET. THE DEGREE OF OVERLAP
INDICATES THE EXTENT OF SHARED OR OVERLAPPING ACTIVITY.
RELATIVE SIZE CAN REFLECT MAGNITUDE, OR THE RELATIVE
IMPORTANCE ATTRIBUTED TO ENTITIES BY THE DRAUGHTSMAN.

Figure 4.5   The Venn diagram convention

Figure 4.5 shows how the Venn diagram might be used to examine the structure of the British economy within the EEC. The 'sets' overlap in some cases, and if we wish to we could adjust the relative areas of the sectors to show their sizes.

However, frequently we are less sure about the structure or relationships being examined. When this is so it is helpful to use a modified form of the Venn diagram, the systems map. This follows the convention by using nested and overlaid shapes but instead of formal squares and rectangles we use the softer 'cloud' or 'blob' shapes. Because the shape is less formal it is easier to question and revise. This diagramming convention thus lends itself to use in group

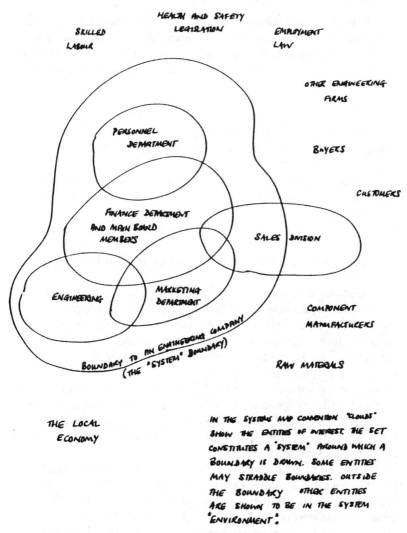

SKILLED
LABOUR

HEALTH AND SAFETY
LEGISLATION

EMPLOYMENT
LAW

OTHER ENGINEERING
FIRMS

PERSONNEL
DEPARTMENT

BUYERS

CUSTOMERS

FINANCE DEPARTMENT
AND MAIN BOARD
MEMBERS

SALES DIVISION

ENGINEERING

MARKETING
DEPARTMENT

COMPONENT
MANUFACTURERS

BOUNDARY TO AN ENGINEERING COMPANY
(THE "SYSTEM" BOUNDARY)

RAW MATERIALS

THE LOCAL
ECONOMY

IN THE SYSTEMS MAP CONVENTION "CLOUDS"
SHOW THE ENTITIES OF INTEREST. THE SET
CONSTITUTES A "SYSTEM" AROUND WHICH A
BOUNDARY IS DRAWN. SOME ENTITIES
MAY STRADDLE BOUNDARIES. OUTSIDE
THE BOUNDARY OTHER ENTITIES
ARE SHOWN TO BE IN THE SYSTEM
"ENVIRONMENT".

Figure. 4.6   The systems map diagramming convention

discussion as well as for individual use. In this context the term 'system' implies organized entities and 'wholes' made up from constituent parts or elements, which themselves may be 'sub-systems'. Outside the boundary lie other elements and systems which make up the environment of the systems you have chosen to represent. In the convention these parts are not enclosed in 'blobs' or 'clouds' in order to distinguish them from the system being depicted. The use of the term 'map' simply conveys the sense of a guide to or summary of information – which is exactly what a good diagram should be. An example of a systems map is shown in Figure 4.6.

Exercise 4.2

Examine the systems map in Figure 4.6 and then try out the diagrammimg convention for yourself using your own family or office as a example.

Try several different groupings until you have developed a satisfactory representation of the structure of your family members or office staff.

Multiple cause diagrams: a powerful analytical tool

Any technique which can be used to explore the dynamic behaviour of some setting will complement the techniques introduced above, which are capable of showing only structure and relationships. The multiple cause diagram can show events and causality. Both concrete and abstract ideas can be combined on a single figure, giving us a powerful but simple diagnostic tool

As a device for note-taking while reading it can be useful as a means of building up an image of the reasons underlying particular events. And as with all good diagramming techniques the organization of the information into a single coherent whole makes it easy to remember and reconstruct.

One of the important features of the multiple cause diagram is that it allows you to show the chains of reasoning behind events, as illustrated in Figure 4.7. But to use the technique to best effect you will need to take some care with the choice of terms at the head and tail of each arrow. A brief phrase containing a verb helps the reader to understand your diagram. Thus the phrase 'sales of widgets decline as market saturates', or even 'sales decline', is more useful to the reader than 'poor sales'. You can think of the use of arrows, lines and boxes, together with the labels, as adding up to the grammar of individual diagramming conventions.

Note that with this technique the arrows mean 'lead to' or 'result in'. Some people think of the diagram as being one which shows 'consequences'. The phrases or labels are used to describe events or activities within the diagram and have a structure of their own. Each phrase should contain a verb and it is useful to qualify each statement with an adjective or adverb to make the meaning clear, e.g. 'many redundancies announced' or 'new branches open'. It is also useful to think of these diagrams as including a 'cast' of characters. Try to include individuals and categories of staff by name if possible. You can see something of this in Figure 4.7.

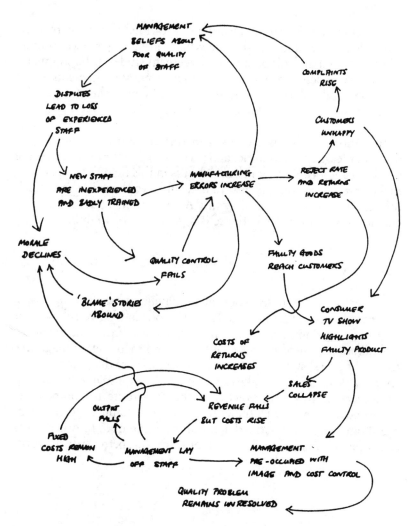

Figure 4.7 The multiple cause diagram used to describe the collapse of an engineering company

Exercise 4.3

Examine Figure 4.7 and then use the same convention to describe the recent history of your own firm, branch or office.

Alternatively, you might like to try to map out the reasons underpinning some decision which you have made recently. Your decision to study this book and other courses?

Of all the diagramming techniques presented in this chapter the multiple cause diagram is the one which, in my experience, is most readily learned and adopted by management students. Its simplicity and ability to describe processes and to incorporate statements about emotions and subjective aspects of a problem make it especially attractive to the most reluctant 'diagrammer'.

From among the ideas presented in this chapter try to select and master at least one technique, and then make it your own. There are few hard and fast rules or dos and don'ts in this field. Be prepared to make several versions of any figure, and avoid having too much information on any one diagram. A maximum of ten or twelve entities or statements to a figure is a good rule of thumb.

Summary

Whether or not you see yourself as having good drawing skills, persevere with diagramming. It is a good and powerful way of summarizing complex issues and arguments. From the range of techniques presented in this chapter – mind maps, spray diagrams, fish-tail figures, systems maps and multiple cause diagrams – try to choose at least one and make it your own. As with so many tools and techniques of this kind practice is the only route to competence. When possible return to the exercises in this chapter and try them again, and apply the same diagramming techniques to other issues and topics as they arise, either in your studies or, better still, at work.

5
Reading Techniques

We now turn to the key skill of reading, and where the ideas concerning memory and diagramming presented in earlier chapters can help to improve reading speed and recall. There are many schemes for speed reading and effective reading, but unfortunately some of them seem to suggest that slow reading is in some way natural. In fact a more likely explanation of slow reading is the poor teaching of reading at an early age. Many reading schemes for children are still based on letter recognition and on phonic techniques for sounding individual words. Unfortunately, these bear little relationship to the use of reading as a skill in later life, and all too frequently we continue to read as adults by looking at the individual word and not at entire groups of words and phrases.

Speed reading has long been one of the most popular study skills and remains so today, but even the most expensive of these 'improve your mind' courses are based on a few simple ideas to do with training yourself to read by using more efficient eye movements. Improving your reading speed can be simple, straightforward and effective.

In these final chapters we will examine these rules and suggestions for speed reading and then go on to examine the tasks associated with planning and preparing essays and reports, which will figure in any course leading to a qualification. Even if you do not see yourself studying for a qualification remember that the skills of report-writing and communication are vital skills for the practising manager. The advice in the next few pages can be applied to your world of work tomorrow . . . if you choose.

Keywords and highlighting

One of the simplest ways of improving your reading speed, comprehension and recall is by using a highlighter or pencil to mark up the text which you are reading. For many this still seems difficult, particularly in books. Traditionally we were taught at school that books were to be regarded as items to be treasured and used by successive generations of children. Many people still regard books as valuable and highly prized possessions. If instead we treat books as consumable items of personal property, annotation and highlighting can only improve their value, for the highlighting and comments in the margin will draw attention immediately to those sections which are most relevant to you.

This book is printed with wider margins and a generous layout in order to encourage annotation. In this way it can be used as a work book and will eventually contain your notes as well, placing your own interpretation on the text and emphasizing the points you consider to be important. Keywords and your own examples can be entered in the margins and will help you when you come to revise the material. Any book you use in your studies can be treated in the same way. Reading and annotating can in this sense be seen as 'consuming' a book.

Speed reading

The eye is capable of scanning lines of text rapidly. As we read the eye scans lines of text from left to right and an average person will usually be able to read approximately 250 words per minute if the material is light and well written. A child learning to read uses a different process which focuses · on the individual word. Unfortunately, few of us are taught to read by scanning the text, and hence the possibility of changing from reading word by word at a rate of perhaps 100 words per minute to scan reading at perhaps 500 words per minute is never appreciated or used. Luckily most of us learn to read rapidly in a line-by-line fashion, but without realizing that we can read faster still by improving the way in which our eyes scan and sample a page of printed text.

Faster speeds depend taking in 'chunks' of text at a time. Whole phrases and lines can be taken in and even higher speeds can be achieved by scanning the text rapidly in a top to bottom manner, picking out key words and phrases. At this rate we are then relying on the ability of the mind to integrate and organize the information, instead of taking the meaning directly from the individual words in the text.

Newspapers with the multiple-column layout lend themselves to this kind of reading. For instead of scanning with left-to-right eye movements we are able to scan vertically in a steady sweep from top to bottom. As you practise your reading try to employ this technique with ordinary text and scan the page from top to bottom instead of from left to right.

Exercise 5.1

The short article below examines the business recovery of Jaguar Cars in the period from 1980 to 1984 in the run up to the (re)privatization of the company.

Time yourself reading it and then calculate your reading speed. The article contains approximately 1,200 words.

At a reading speed of 250 words per minute it should take under five minutes. At double that speed, 500 words per minute, a speed you should be able to reach with practice, it would take less than three minutes.

This test will set a baseline from which you can measure your progress.

QUALITY BRINGS SALES DIVIDENDS AT JAGUAR

Geoffrey Hancock

(Reprinted from *Quality Progress*, pp. 30-3, American Society for Quality Control. Reprinted with permission.)

When John Egan joined Jaguar in April 1980 as chairman and chief executive losses had been running at about $3 million a month. The situation was grave. His brief from the British Leyland parent board was blunt - either stop the losses and get on a profit course or close the business. Under Egan's direction Jaguar set about developing a quality control programme intended to turn the business around. Now nearly four years later, the dramatic effect of that programme can be seen in Jaguar sales, the raising of morale, and the boost to wages.

Egan explains: 'I knew we had a beautiful world class car but I also knew we had to introduce improvements to our quality.' He sought those improvements by what he called 'the pursuit of perfection'. This effort dealt with identified quality problems and has since been developed to take in all aspects of efficiency in the Jaguar operation. The effect has been electric. Jaguar is booming again and making a profit. This surplus is hidden in the overall BL (British Leyland) accounts, but the Jaguar operation today has a considerable degree of independence.

The quality factor has been reflected in the rise–fall–rise of Jaguar sales figures, from 1976 to 1983. These figures are eloquent testimony to the dividends paid by attention to quality. For hardly any other reason could world sales of Jaguar cars in 1983 have shown such a marked increase over the previous year.

The most outstanding increase was in North America, where the total sales of 16,000 cars were more than 5000 higher than in 1982. US sales of 15,815 put Jaguar Cars Inc. 50% above the previous record annual sales total of 10,349 set in 1982.

The first step in Jaguar's turnaround came when it identified 150 problems related to quality, 60 per cent of them the responsibility of outside suppliers and the rest occurring 'in house' with factory-prepared components and assembly. Task forces were organized and each was given responsibility for curing specific faults.

One problem, involving front disc brake noise and vibration, was identified through high warranty costs and customer complaints. The appropriate task force set about diagnosing the problem, finding a remedy and then implementing it. As a result the specification of the brake pad was changed; a new source found for the disc casting; and new equipment at Jaguar's Radford factory produced matched sets of discs to much finer tolerances. Also, to protect the disc assemblies from water and grit during transit, it was decided to protect them with plastic bags.

The task force concept proved important when in 1980, Jaguar became the owner of the former Pressed Steel Fisher assembly plant and paint shop, and inherited some long established paint problems. Another Jaguar task force found that the problems arose with the thermoplastic reflow system. This system was revised and re-equipped and the workforce retrained; the effort paid off with significant improvements.

Between its worst year and the start of its revival in 1982, Jaguar dispensed with 40 component suppliers who were unable, or unwilling, to provide the quality demanded. During this period the company placed the financial onus on its suppliers and made them pay the cost of work arising from their quality failures. The success of this scheme led to the introduction of the Jaguar warranty threshold policy, under which the supplier assumes liability for all labour, handling and costs when the fault incidence exceeds 1.5 per cent. By the end of 1984, the suppliers of 73 per cent (by value) of the components will have joined the scheme.

Jaguar's philosophy now is to take its association with suppliers beyond a purely commercial relationship. It aims to develop a long term relationship and encourage research and development. At regular meetings, Jaguar engineers and the suppliers work towards a situation in which the suppliers warrant their products as being 'fit for purchase and use'.

Suppliers are now graded on the 'fitness for purpose' standard. After a complete audit, they are adjudged either to be first class in every respect of quality, system and procedures or to meet most requirements, although some areas still need remedial treatment or to be suitable for a business action programme which will either move the firm to one of the higher categories or lead Jaguar to find a new source for the component.

Jaguar's new approach helped to solve a problem with power steering faults that had been traced to oil seal leakage. The supplier had difficulty in eliminating the fault and so Jaguar engineering and quality personnel moved into that factory, helping the company to revise the complete manufacturing process and working jointly on a new and higher specification for assembly.

In some cases it was not easy to establish where remedial action was needed, and so customer tracking proved useful. Telephone calls were made to 150 Jaguar buyers in the US and 150 buyers in Britain, and were followed up after 30 days and again after nine months. One point that emerged was the surprisingly high number of owners experiencing headlamp-bulb failures. This had not showed up in warranty returns for the simple reason that dealers had replaced the faulty bulbs without claiming for the new ones. As a result of the calls to customers, the bulb fault was referred back to the supplier, who took action to improve quality.

Quality also comes into the reckoning in the standard of dealerships, of which Jaguar has about 200 in the US. As Neil Johnson, Jaguar's director of sales and marketing, explains, dealers are very often the only point of contact with customers, and looking after Jaguar customers is a highly specialized job.

Like many other car firms, Jaguar has to part company with dealers from time to time, although in the US terminations have been counterbalanced by new signings. Decisions to end agreements are based on assessments that suggest minimum standards have not been met and are unlikely to be achieved. In Britain in the past few years Jaguar terminated agreements with dealers that had not come up to expectations, but some 220 other dealers met the standards required.

Jaguar's success is, in large part, because during the most severe part of a worldwide trade depression, the company was able to motivate a dispirited workforce to join in a concerted effort to put matters right at Jaguar. During a two-year period, Jaguar's payroll was reduced at all levels by 30 per cent. Nevertheless, both quality and productivity rose during that period. The upshot is that while 10,500 employees made 14,105 cars in 1980 only 7,400 employees produced 22,046 cars in 1982. And the 28,000 cars built in 1983 are the most Jaguar has produced since 1974.

Your reading of the brief article on Jaguar should have left you with several key points: Egan's role, quality, suppliers, commitment, task force and productivity. If you doubt this check it again and highlight these points.

You will find it helpful to think of reading in three basic ways. I call them 'skim-reading', 'scan-reading' and 'critical reading'. Or, if you wish, a high, mid and low gear, with the low gear – critical reading – being reserved for the really difficult going.

From now on try to ensure that you read as a conscious active exercise. Try to avoid simply opening a book and settling down to read in a casual fashion. Make sure that you either read slowly and deliberately by choice, a tactic which can be sensible and appropriate if you are dealing with a complex text; or decide to speed-read by scanning for phrases and entire lines. The basic technique of speed reading involves training yourself to read entire phrases and lines instead of the individual words.

If you have a long text to work through always try to skim-read it first by turning the pages noting the titles and contents to get an idea of the structure and layout, then scan-read by making your eyes deliberately scan each page from top to bottom and, finally, if necessary, return to any difficult passages and read these deliberately – critical reading. Note-taking can accompany either the second or third phases if you wish to have your own record of the main ideas in a piece of text.

Note-taking and summarizing

Whatever the nature and structure of the course you plan to take there will be numerous occasions when note-taking will be an important skill. Lectures, work with case-study video material and the revision of set texts are just a few examples of the situations when you will need an efficient, accurate and simple method for note-taking.

Written notes

Handwritten notes will always be useful for revision and for checking your understanding of any passage of text. Decide for yourself whether identifying the key points only will be sufficient.

If more elaborate notes including summaries of arguments, etc. are needed, you may wish to use 'bullet' points and to organize your remarks under a series of headings.

Many students find that the exercise of rewriting notes at a later date enables them to clarify their understanding of text and to reinforce the learning, as we saw in the example in Chapter 3 of the performance of Australian university students. Rewriting notes can also improve their clarity and layout and thus improve their value as a revision tool.

Diagrams

As we saw in the preceding chapter diagrams are a powerful tool for organizing and taking notes. If you decide to use them select a technique with which you are familiar and then use it consistently. In this way you will improve your skill in diagramming and find that you can expand the diagramming convention by inventing your own notation.

Exercise 5.2

Return to the article in Exercise 5.1 describing quality control at Jaguar. Read through it again, and then use a mind map to record the main points.

Now read it again more carefully, making notes. Put your mind map away first.

Finally, compare your mind map with your written notes and try to decide which is more suitable for you.

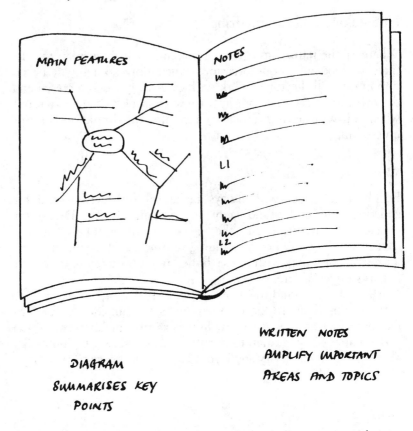

Figure 5.1   A two-page layout for combining written notes with diagrams

You may in the end decide that a combination of notes and diagrams suits best of all. In this case consider using a separate notebook and laying out your work in the fashion of Figure 5.1. This form of layout is recommended by Buzan (1974) as a comprehensive way of making notes.

Arguments in the written word

One of the problems with many speed-reading techniques is that they take little or no account of the complexity of the text. In the course of your studies you will come across complex arguments.

Unfortunately, this will sometimes be in badly written material but on other occasions it will be because the line of reasoning is indeed just difficult. Some ideas are difficult to express in words and few people are able to put complex notions into simple language.

When faced with this challenge you will have to dissect the text and seek out the main points and then look for the evidence presented in support of them. This process of critical reading is an important skill, for you should be able to test the validity of any author's argument by the quality of the evidence presented. Think of yourself as a detective looking for evidence, and ask a series of questions which may yield some helpful clues:

1. What is the main point being made by the author?
2. What evidence is offered?
3. What are the subsidiary points?
4. What kind of evidence is being offered? Is it subjective, or based on fact?

Facts and assertions

When analysing text you will need to distinguish between facts and assertions. Is the statement backed up by evidence? Is it supported by references which are cited. Are examples offered? If so do you believe them?

Assertions are unsupported statements, claims or opinions and are, as such, open to challenge. It may be that your knowledge as a reader supports the claim; inevitably, all authors make assumptions about the knowledge of their expected readers. Do you agree with the views expressed? If so, why?

This distinction is especially important in management education, where there is often only weak evidence to support claims. As you read more about the practice of management you will become aware that much of the evidence offered is in the form of examples of 'good' and 'bad' practice. Invariably these judgements will be subjective so that, as a reader, you will have to form a view on any such claims.

Evidence: primary and secondary sources and the case study

In any text you should try to distinguish between primary sources, which support a claim directly, and secondary sources, which are one stage removed. For example, the report of a piece of market research on a product may be quoted directly, i.e. as a primary source. On the other hand, the author may be citing the findings indirectly, in the sense of 'it is reported that market research has shown . . .'. These are secondary sources. After all, the author of a text which uses secondary sources is accepting the original evidence on face value and may even be misinterpreting the findings of the first author.

The difficulty of relating research to practice in management has given rise to a unique form of evidence in this field: the case study. First introduced at the Harvard Business School, the case study is the dominant source of information in management education. For example, the Cranfield School of Management maintains its own register or clearing house of case studies for its students, researchers and clients.

Good, well-prepared case studies provide an insight into the personalities and inner workings of an organization. This allows the management student to understand and interpret the material in terms of his or her own organization.

Case studies are very widely used in management development and you should endeavour to develop your own way of analysing them. Case-study writers usually try to be objective but their enthusiasm for individuals or for styles of management inevitably biases the presentation. Try to identify bias and to look beyond it into the evidence presented and use this as your guide for any conclusions you may wish to draw on company X or Y, or on management technique A or B. Remember that in any discussion or debate you will need to marshall your evidence in support of any points you may wish to make. Evidence from relevant case-study examples may be the best source if you are to convince your fellow managers. In general they are much more likely to be convinced by evidence based on the successful application of ideas than evidence based only on the ideas and theory.

Exercise 5.3

Allow about one hour for this exercise.

The extracts reprinted below are from an article entitled 'Morality at boardroom level' by Jack Mahoney, which appeared in the *Times Higher Education Supplement* on 5 May 1989. It concerns the emergence of business ethics as a topic of debate and as a subject to be taught in management schools.

Read the article, making notes as you go in a manner and style of your own choosing.

MORALITY AT BOARDROOM LEVEL

Jack Mahoney

(The author is the F. D. Maurice professor of moral and social theology at King's College, London. He is the director of the King's College Business Ethics Research Centre, which he founded in 1987.)

The term business ethics conveys a variety of meanings. Some people greet it with a raised eyebrow and a murmured, 'surely a contradiction in terms?' More commonly, others connect it with the increasingly public concern for ethical standards of behaviour in business. In the academic context, however, 'business ethics' refers to the new field of systematic study which has blossomed remarkably in the past 20 years in the United States, and is now slowly beginning to develop in Britain and the rest of Europe.

The development of modern business ethics in the United States since the 1960s stems from the cumulative effect on an American conscience shaken by Watergate and Vietnam of the disclosure of massive bribery on the part of major business corporations; the powerful campaigns against racial and sexual discrimination at work and in the market place; growing sensitivity to consumer and public safety and to environmental values; and a mounting concern spearheaded by the churches for the plight of the poor at home and in the third world. As a consequence, American society began to articulate for business what one observer calls a 'changing social mandate', to question its traditional myth of rugged frontier individualism and its single minded pursuit of the bottom line.

Support for this endeavour came in terms of experience and motivation from the business community itself, in a blend of awakened social responsibility, old-fashioned American philanthropy, and enlightened self-protection. The major intellectual input, however, came from the academic, and notably the philosophical, community as a further extension of the resurgence in the United States of applied ethics, or of what one writer identified as 'the rebirth of ethics'.

Not all academics were in sympathy with what some saw as a fashionable and distasteful descent into the market place. Others, however, view the move as a socially responsible and constructive contribution to public and moral reflection, and one which has been legitimated and stimulated by the work of such respected thinkers as Macintyre and Rawls. Moreover, precedents had already been set in the public contributions of philosophers and religious thinkers in such fields as nuclear deterrence, legal ethics and most of all in medical ethics. The number and scale of the ethical options arising from the rapid expansion of medical technology and bureaucracy had led to often vocal but confused public debates in this field and this offered a whole new outlet for religious and philosophical thinkers to bring clarity and consistency to such debates. It was a logical extension of such public involvement in the American scene for the academic community to enter into comparable debates arising from the vastly increased resources and powers for good or ill of modern business corporations.

Courses, conferences and specialized centres rapidly developed, together with a growing body of literature, to give shape to the new discipline of Business Ethics.

Concepts and terminology were explored, arguments expounded and examined, presuppositions uncovered, and the agenda of the new discipline progressively identified. The results can be seen in the topics chosen for successive regional and national conferences, and in the volumes of the *Journal of Business Ethics*, which began as a quarterly in 1982 and has recently begun to appear monthly.

As a consequence today in America business ethics is well established as an academic field of study, teaching and research. It is highly fashionable, and yet all the signs are that it is not just another passing fad. Whether it is succeeding and, for that matter, what is to count as success is another matter. It is also big business, as the development of ethical consultants and the $30 million grant made last year to develop business ethics programmes at the Harvard Business School make abundantly clear.

In Britain, the business, and indeed the academic, scenes could not be unaffected by such transatlantic developments. But the growing concern here for ethical behaviour in business, and the growing interest in developing business ethics as an academic discipline, cannot be dismissed simply as an instance of our catching one of America's colds 10 years later. The social concerns which in the United States gave rise to putting human and social values firmly on the business agenda and to submitting business practice to increasing public scrutiny can be paralleled by native growths here, which require chronicling and are daily gathering momentum.

The increased interest on the part of major companies in

introducing or updating corporate credos or mission statements and codes of conduct, and the moves to professionalize business and management with codes of good practice, reflect a genuine upsurge of social responsibility within the British business community. And the initiatives which are being taken in business schools and university and polytechnic departments in Britain appear to be both articulating and responding to the increased social awareness of moral responsibilities of business in contemporary society. [. . .]

[. . .] The signs are, however, that in Britain as in the rest of the continent, business ethics is becoming a modest academic growth industry as demand and enterprise grow together, the market is slowly being identified or created, and resources develop to meet demand.

One practical indication is the number of exploratory seminars or round-tables being held on the subject, as at Warwick and Hull. Another is the growing number of specialized 'centres' which are developing to business ethics, either in its own right, or from a particular religious standpoint, or as part of a wider social agenda, as in Manchester, Edinburgh, Oxford and Cambridge.

Those involved in teaching the new discipline, as at the London Business School, are aware of formidable curricular, methodological and teaching challenges. For one thing, the available literature for teaching basic courses is largely American and naturally concentrates on the American business scene and on American cases.

British texts such as those by Goyder and Handy, are valuable in general terms, but the works of Beauchamp and Bowie and more recently of Donaldson and Werhane, standard in American colleges and universities, are indispensable for a systematic approach to modern issues. Studies based on the British experience, however, are shortly to appear from the Strathclyde Business School and from Imperial College London, and others are in preparation which will begin to apply ethical reflection and principles in the British context.

Given the preferred method of teaching business and management studies in general by case studies, largely under the influence of the Harvard tradition, the lack of literature applying ethical analysis to the British and European scenes is also a serious deficiency, although this too is gradually being addressed.

The method to be adopted in teaching business ethics raises three questions which are interlinked: the approach to the subject, the place of the subject in the curriculum, and the teaching resources in the subject. There is a long running debate in the United States about the comparative advantages and disadvantages of approaching the subject of business ethics from individual cases to the general principles, or by starting from principles to apply them to particular situations.

[. . .] In these three methodological areas of approach, place and teaching resources in the development of business ethics a useful precedent may be available in the similar debates which have been occupying the medical schools in regard to the study and teaching of medical ethics.

The Pond report on the teaching of medical ethics (1987) acknowledged a wide disparity of practice, but observed that 'medical ethics is central to the practice of medicine and its implications should be made explicit throughout medical education'. In order to bring this about it recommended, *inter alia*, that medical ethics teaching should occur regularly, should be allotted explicit space in the teaching process, and should normally begin from discussion of particular cases supported by relevant papers.

Its solution to the problem of providing ethical expertise depended heavily on regular multidisciplinary teaching as being advantageous not only to students but also to teachers. And it made the important observation that while ethical considerations should enter into every phase of medical education 'some opportunity should be provided for ethical reflection on themes common to all the specialities'.

Finally, there is the all-important area of the content of the business ethics courses. Major issues which occupy centre stage in the United States include the nature of corporate, as distinct from individual, responsibility; management roles and relationships; the implications of the new 'stakeholder' concept to embrace all in the community who have a stake in how a company conducts its business; and the phenomenon of 'corporate' culture.

On the whole, though with various exceptions, the tendency is to ignore the macro-issues of economics and to concentrate on practical ethical behaviour within the existing capitalist and free market systems.

A British, and European, approach to the subject, however, could scarcely ignore alternative economic systems and structures, and their implications for the conduct of business. Nor could it fail to take serious account of such groundwork issues as the ethics of competition and its varied consequences, the ethics of share ownership, the competing cases for deregulation, self-regulation and legislation, and, pervading all, the ethics of self-interest and of economic and social individualism.

Commenting last year on the growing academic initiative in business ethics in Britain, John Lloyd wrote realistically, but partially, in the *Financial Times*: 'The professors need business because they need to fund their colleges in an era of state withdrawal: and the business people need the professors because they must find an ethic for the greater role they are being asked to play – and which they themselves are proposing for themselves – in society.'

The matter could also be expressed in less economic terms as a recognition that the academic community has more to offer the business community and today's 'enterprise culture' in general, than scientific and technical advances and expertise, valuable as these are. The humanities too have an important contribution to make in supporting business to find its role as an integral part of a humane society which can truly flourish only in terms of the life-quality of all its members.

If that view be greeted cynically, as the term 'business ethics' itself sometimes is, the answer must lie in a due appreciation of the age-old phenomenon with which business itself is not unacquainted, that of mixed motives for morally good behaviour.

Now ask yourself:

1. What facts and assertions are presented?
2. What evidence is offered to support the author's views or claims?
3. Is the style of writing objective?
4. Is the writer trying to be informative or is he trying to persuade you to adopt a particular view on issues?

In all your future study of articles and case studies try to keep these questions in mind.

Your study of this article should have revealed important lessons about this kind of writing. Clearly the author has a detailed knowledge of business ethics. The paper is full of information about the background to the topic and about current developments.

How can we judge whether the material is accurate? Are the views expressed solely those of the author? Is any evidence presented to back up his claims about ethics in management? Most readers tend to assume that any statement in an article of this kind is true. Did you?

These remarks should serve to illustrate a central point in dealing with written material in your course work: always try to assess the material critically, by looking for evidence to back up any claims or assertions, and be prepared to be sceptical and challenging. Because so much of management education is based on case-study material you must also be prepared to cross-check and re-examine the validity of claims which attempt to generalize from specific examples or cases.

Try to use the suggestions here and the earlier questions to sharpen up your reading of management texts. Try to adopt a critical style in your reading and to analyse the style of writing and arguments being used. The same approach can also be applied to documents and reports internal to your own company. Is someone trying to sell a particular line of development without offering any supporting evidence?

Summary

Reading forms a central part of any form of study, and although well-designed management courses place considerable emphasis on practical exercises and simulations, you will never remove the need for reading. Of course the same is true of much managerial work. So once again we find that a study skill can be transferred directly into the workplace. In this chapter speed reading and various ways of making notes have been introduced. Try them out until you settle into a method which suits your way of working.

Most important is the ability to read material critically, searching out the main arguments and the way in which evidence and information are marshalled within a piece of writing. Don't take everything at face value whether it be a journal article or a business report.

6

Writing and Preparing Reports

Outlining and planning

Any course of study for credit or qualification will require you to prepare assignments and reports. Experience suggests that many managers are by disposition happier 'up and doing' rather than sitting and writing. Thus you are not unusual or atypical if you find it difficult to sit and compose reports. Indeed many successful managers openly admit to a fear and dislike of report-writing. Nevertheless, for any course work it is a task which has to be done. Here we are concerned with ways of making that more attractive, easier and more satisfying.

Writing starts with planning and outlining. Very few people are able to write well without a considerable period of reflection and planning. 'Displacement activities' as you prepare to write are not entirely wasteful for this very reason. Frequently the delay and difficulty in starting merely reflect the lack of organization in your thinking about the chosen topic.

There are several simple ways of planning and organizing an essay. Notes and headings on cards or Post-it pads will allow you to sort and resort your ideas. Figures such as mind maps, spray diagrams and multiple cause diagrams may help you to see the links between sets of ideas.

Reading and revising any background material should complement these tasks and help to pinpoint evidence and references you may wish to use.

Some general guidelines on assignments and reports

The most useful advice for organizing written work follows from the standard dictum for speech writers: say what you are going to say, say it, say what you've said. For report-writing this translates into a simple structure for most pieces of work:

1. a summary;
2. an introduction;
3. the main body of your argument organized into sections with subheadings or by paragraphs;
4. conclusions.

The instructions for any assignment will usually contain some advice about the use of subheadings. In conventional essays headings in the text are inappropriate, but in management reports they are an important feature signalling to your reader that a new topic is about to be addressed. Anyone skimming through the report is able to get an overview of the argument quickly and, most important, can see the logic and structure of the report at a glance. There will be occasions where it is appropriate to number the paragraphs and sections of a report. For example, a document to be laid before a committee for discussion will be helped by a clear simple numbering system for paragraphs. In your management studies there may well be assignments of this kind for you to prepare. If in doubt seek advice from your tutor – the course or college may well have its own guidelines for reports and assignments. Government reports have a numbering system for paragraphs which runs from the start to finish. Obviously the numbers run into the hundreds in major reports, but it provides a simple indexing system independent of page numbers. In your more modest course work the same applies: don't be tempted into new numbering systems for different sections or chapters unless you are specifically directed to do so.

At the end of your assignment your conclusions should follow from the logic of any analysis presented in the body of the assignment or report.

Above all, aim for clarity of presentation in your written material. Avoid lengthy sentences and complex grammatical structures – aim for plain English.

Using notes and references

For major reports and projects you will have to keep track of a great deal of information. File cards are a convenient way of maintaining references by author and subject. This kind of simple database is most useful when maintained consistently. It can then serve to show up otherwise forgotten or overlooked connections between topics.

If file cards require organization and management, rough notes lie at the other extreme. If you see yourself as hopelessly disorganized don't despair: for you, rough notes on a scrap of paper may be sufficient as a trigger to your thinking. The plan of the essay will then have to be carried in your head. This works well for many but places some constraints on timing. Good ideas will evaporate unless you are able to set them down on paper promptly. A detailed essay plan will, in contrast, allow you to put aside the task and return to it later without having to start again from scratch.

The layout and accuracy of your references are important in both technical reports and in management writings. There are several ways of organizing and setting out references. Footnotes allow the reader to pick up points of detail and references without turning to the back of an essay or report, but it is more common to find references cited by year or numbered in the text and listed in detail at the back of a report. Thus you might find: 'as stated by Another (3) in the 1986 study' or 'Another (1986) states that . . .'. This reference, if it related to a journal article, would then be listed at the end of an assignment as:

Another, A. B. 'Coals to Newcastle', *Journal of Mining*, **12** (1986), 55–66

or, as in this book for example:

Another, A. B. (1986) Coals to Newcastle, *Journal of Mining*, Vol. 12, pp. 55–66.

In printed texts book and journal titles are frequently set in italic and the volume number of a journal in bold type (as in the examples above), but in your handwritten or typed reports such attention to detail cannot be expected. Where books are referred to take care to include the publisher and edition if appropriate; there is nothing more infuriating than to check a reference only to find that you have insufficient information or, worse, that part of the information is wrong.

You will find that your college or company lays down a separate standard for references, etc. and, if so, you must of course follow it, but the guidelines here are intended to ensure that your references are useful to your readers. In the course of your studies look carefully at the way in which these questions of design and layout are managed in the books and case studies which you use; you will then be able to develop your own style for reports and assignments.

Figures and diagrams

There will be many occasions when figures and diagrams, including the various kinds discussed earlier, will be appropriate for your reports. As the saying goes, a picture is worth a thousand words, but take care to refer to your figures and to number them sequentially as you write out your reports. To save time with your assignments it will usually be faster to include diagrams and figures on separate sheets of paper. Don't spend time trying to incorporate them into the text; juggling the sizes and matching these with gaps in your text is difficult – your essay isn't intended to emulate the work of a professional designer and printer. Finally, beware those odd occasions when diagrams are inappropriate, though the only occasion which comes readily to mind is the prepared speech when visual aids are not available. However, there are occasions when you must make your prose do all the work, unsupported by figures and diagrams. It is then that a clear and simple style with well-presented arguments will gain you good grades.

Drafting

When the planning is over it is time to start writing. As you start to write do not worry unduly about style, punctuation and grammar. Instead concentrate on getting the ideas down on paper. A handwritten essay may require two or three drafts before you feel it is in good shape so it is important to allow sufficient time for redrafting. Many authors like to leave their material for a short time before redrafting. This is good practice, for ambiguities and poor structure will become much easier to spot and correct if you are returning to it fresh.

Start with your main headings and under these add subheadings and begin to jot down your ideas in note form. Very often a spray diagram or similar technique will allow you to organize your ideas for a first draft. Try to order the ideas so that your argument builds up and flows through the assignment.

If you own, or have access to, a word-processor, this phase

becomes much faster and more efficient, though the need to leave the material at times and return to it later is not diminished in any way.

Plain English

Style matters in written work and normally needs to be a compromise between something which is 'you' and the needs of your readers. A plain simple structure will usually serve you well, with paragraphing to separate new arguments as you introduce them.

For many of us grammar becomes an obstacle in written work. Rules from school defy recall and we are left puzzling over spellings and punctuation. There are many sources of help which can sort out the 'its' from the 'it's' and when 'i' comes before 'e'. One such is produced by the Open University for adult students who are returning to study: *Plain English* (Open University, 1984) is a guide to simple grammar and English usage. Alternatively, you should consider purchasing a copy of Ernest Gower's (1971) *Complete Plain Words*. Though this little book was first published in 1948 it has been steadily reprinted ever since and still sells well today in paperback form. Most bookstores will have something to help you. W. H. Smith produces a range of inexpensive pamphlets aimed at children, setting out the rules of grammar and modern usage of English. In addition, a good dictionary and a thesaurus can make writing fun and an activity of discovery. If you begin to take more interest in your writing, the *Oxford Guide to the English Language* (Oxford University Press, 1984) and a dictionary of quotations will complete your armoury.

Redrafting, checking, proofing and references

Between drafts try to get someone else to read your work with a sympathetic eye. Misspellings and obscure usage that are invisible to you will jump off the page to your new reader. Your reader may also be able to suggest improvements in layout, and check the final versions of your report for consistency in your references.

References are the way in which you can introduce evidence to support the argument of your text. There are several conventions for this so you should aim to choose one and stick to it, using the guidelines given earlier to shape your choice. A glance through your study texts will reveal a wide variety of styles. Choose a simple one for the references in your reports and essays; ensure that it is consistent with your aims and, finally, get someone to check them through for accuracy.

Word processing for outlining, drafting and editing

The availability of word processors for little more than the price of an electric typewriter brings them within reach of most managers. Indeed you may find that access to a personal computer (usually compatible with an IBM PC) is required by your college. Many part-time MBA programmes now make this an integral part of the course and extend the use of information technology to include the teaching of financial management, and the use of electronic mail in addition to the more mundane word processing of reports.

If you are prepared to invest your money, first decide if you are also prepared to invest a period of time in learning to use the machine efficiently. Competitive prices in the shops mean that a dealer's margins do not include much in the way of after-sales support. So if the answer is in the manual or handbook you may not receive a sympathetic response to your calls to the shop for help

Many colleges and polytechnics run inexpensive courses for the better-known office standard word-processing software and this may justify investing in a somewhat more expensive machine than the cheapest available so that you can also run industry standard programs. You may even be able to choose a management programme which includes a course introducing the personal computer as a business tool. If you have access to machines in your office it will make sense to buy a compatible machine. You will then be in the enviable position of having an office machine and another at home.

The cost is not limited to the machine; you will have printer, paper, and disks to consider as well, so ownership should be thought through carefully. What uses do you have for a computer beyond word processing? But in report-writing a word processor can give you considerable flexibility and other advantages:

1. layout can be changed;
2. whole paragraphs and blocks of text can be moved around within a document;
3. corrections to spellings and punctuation do not involve retyping the entire report;
4. references can be added or removed at will.

As with all machines there are pitfalls and limitations, of which the most trivial is 'finger trouble' with the keyboard, leading to repeated errors and mistakes. Typing skill can help you master the 'qwerty' keyboard – so called because of the arrangement of keys on the top row of a typewriter but there will still be other dedicated keys to learn on any computer. One-finger typing is perfectly adequate for most occasional users and any errors in the text are easily corrected. In American schools children are taught typewriting, with the result that everyone in an office can use any keyboard machine without difficulty. Compare that with our own English experience and its implications for life in the office.

The most serious problem for the novice user of a word processor is the unintended deletion of your entire report. Most users do this at least once and learn the hard way that there is a value to the habit of making regular back-up copies of your work as writing progresses.

Technical problems usually occur when you are in a hurry or late at night when reports are overdue, but surveys of faults show that almost all 'faults' on modern electronic devices are not 'faults' at all but errors which are made, but not understood, by the operator.

The size of most desk-top machines means that you will need a separate table and, as with all electrical equipment, there is the 'spaghetti' of cables to master. The size and weight of most word processors restrict them to your home or office so the other major drawback is the lack of portability. Lightweight battery-powered 'laptop' machines overcome this, but in the final analysis pen and paper are more flexible and convenient if you are forced to write 'on the move', despite what the advertisers would have us believe.

Grades and continuous assessment

Any reports or assignments prepared as a part of your course will probably be assessed in some way. Do take care to structure your assignment to reflect any marking scheme you have been told about. If most of the marks are allocated to some part of the assignment it makes sense to put in more time on this part of the work.

When the work comes back you will have the opportunity to look for your tutor's advice and guidance on the script. If your grades are good further advice may not be needed, but for B or C grades and worse do make sure that you get some feedback. A good tutor will be able to show you how a question can be tackled from a new angle and how your arguments can be improved. Comparison of your work with that of other members of the course can also be helpful, so do take advantage of any opportunity which may present itself for working with your colleagues on a course.

Summary

The key points to remember in report-writing are:

1. the need for planning ahead of time;
2. the use of notes and diagrams to structure your thinking;
3. the use of headings to structure your assignment;
4. the need for an introduction, argument and conclusion;
5. the need for care with references and figures;
6. the need for a simple clear style; and
7. the assistance of a colleague or friend to read through your work and point out obvious mistakes and misspellings.

7

Managing Yourself

Stress – the phenomenon of the 1990s?

Stress at work and in life in general is now recognized as a major cause of absence from work, poor performance and, in the extreme, as an indirect cause of premature deaths. Yet human resources managers and managers themselves are only just beginning to see stress as something which is avoidable and is in almost all cases manageable. Even at the level when it causes irritability, sleepless nights and a lack of energy, stress may be damaging and it is largely up to you to recognize this and to take steps to control the demands on your time, emotions and energy.

Stress, study and work

In undertaking study in addition to your normal work you will be exposing yourself to the risk of increased stress as heavier demands are made on your time. It is likely that these combined demands will have an effect on your personal life and on other members of your immediate family. Certainly many part-time students find that their studies prevent them from following their normal hobbies and sports, with the result that they are unintentionally depriving themselves of the very activities which enable them to exercise, relax and prepare themselves for working effectively.

More serious is the effect of having one member of a household constantly preoccupied with his or her studies. Ordinary family life will be disrupted unless you are prepared to take steps to deal with this unexpected consequence of returning to study.

These risks imply that the decision to take up a course involves not just the student but also other members of his or her household. Involving others is the first and most important step you can take to assess and reduce the levels of stress associated with trying to combine work, study and family life.

Recognizing stress and the risk of added stress if you are taking on a new project is the first important step in managing yourself. If you are in mid-career it is likely that your work and lifestyle already involve juggling your time between several competing demands. This may lead to stress which can, at times, be damaging. It is well known that certain life events are the most important causes of stress: job changes, promotions, house moves, marriage, divorce and bereavement are all rated as leading causes of stress-related conditions by both the medical profession and occupational psychologists. A heavy and unrelenting workload and poor health can both cause and be aggravated by stress.

Stress is difficult to define adequately and is all too easily seen only in a negative light. It is best understand as a condition which reflects a degree of mismatch or maladaptation between an individual and his or her environment (in the broadest sense of the term) which cannot be compensated for by normal behaviour (as in work, leisure, sleep, relaxation, exercise, etc.). The first thing to appreciate is that our bodies respond to threats and stimuli by producing adrenalin – the flight or fight reaction. This natural and valuable mechanism is also involved in stress. Indeed stress and the feelings of exhaustion, lassitude and inability to cope can be described as the result of the body's continued attempts to respond to new challenges. Figure 7.1 shows how the response can be either one of coping and managing or one of stress.

The idea of mismatch is important for it suggests that the causes of stress, be they physical or psychological, can be identified and therefore be either reduced or removed.

The symptoms of stress are many and varied. It may manifest itself in feelings of inadequacy, fatigue, of 'not coping', irritability or in more serious medical conditions. Here we are not concerned with conditions which require medical help – if you are in any doubt then seek medical advice. Instead this chapter is intended to give you some understanding of the causes, risks and symptoms of stress so that you can avoid becoming a victim and learn to manage stress and to prevent it becoming an obstacle in your studies.

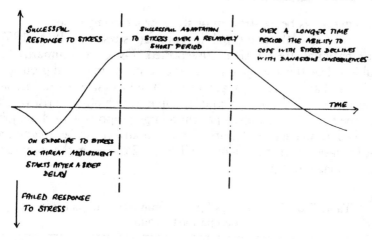

Figure 7.1 Responses to challenges: coping with stress

Occupations and stress

There is a broad relationship between occupation and stress, with certain groups – especially those professions involving responsibility and care for people, such as nursing, teaching and the police –

Table 7.1 Stress ratings for occupational groups

Occupational group	Average stress rating for group (0 to 10 scale)
Uniformed professions	6.4
Commerce/management	5.3
Arts and communication	5.3
Industrial production	5.1
Caring professions (teacher, etc.)	4.7
Health	4.6
Personal services (hotels, etc.)	4.5
Public service industries	4.5
Professional services (law, etc.)	4.4
Environment	4.2
Public administration	4.2
Financial areas	4.0
Technical specialists	3.7

Source: HMSO (1987, part 1)

showing up as being stressful or stress-prone occupations.

In a series of recent publications on stress (HMSO, 1987) 'occupational stress' ratings are reported. These are summarized in Table 7.1 as the average ratings for certain occupational groups.

From Table 7.1 it is apparent that the highest stress ratings are associated with the occupational group in which physical risks exist, but the next three groups represent a large proportion of those jobs labelled as managerial. Clearly, being a manager can be stressful, as the breakdown of these figures in Table 7.2 reveals in the commerce and management group.

Table 7.2   Stress ratings for the commerce and management
occupational group

Commerce and management	Average stress rating for group (0 to 10 scale)
Advertising	7.3
Personnel	6.0
Management	5.8
Marketing/export	5.8
Public relations	5.8
Sales and retailing	5.7
Company secretary	5.3
Secretary	4.7
Purchasing and supply	4.5
Market research	4.3
Work study/O & M	3.6

Source: HMSO (1987, part 1)

Even within this grouping we can see wide variations, with advertising rating at 7.3, a score which places it close to the rating for police (7.7) and journalism (7.5). But the overall message is clear: for the manager stress goes with the job, so managing stress is a skill which any manager should try to acquire simply in order to protect his or her health and maintain the quality of life.

The positive side of stress

We all experience and need some degree of stress, and for some individuals (often termed Type B people – see below) of a placid, equable disposition it is rarely a cause for concern. The physiological mechanisms which enable us to cope with physical danger and extreme emotion are involved in stress. These are mechanisms which enable the body to release a burst of adrenalin in 'flight or fight' situations. They are valuable and are also involved in the feelings of excitement and urgency that give people in many walks of life a sense of being needed in a valuable and worthwhile job.

Yet these same mechanisms can be the cause of problems to some people. One popular school of thought classifies individuals into Type A and Type B people (Type A individuals, the busy, restless, hyperactive types and Type B milder, equable people). This classification emerged from a long study of heart disease, and showed that behaviour was very important (see, e.g., Cooper, Cooper and Eaker, 1988, pp. 47–55).

Some individuals of Type A cope well under continuous pressure, indeed they seem to thrive and statistics suggest that they do not experience ill-health or reduced life expectancy, but some Type As seem to be prone to stress-related problems. In contrast, Type B people are more equable and are less easily roused. But the Type A individuals as a group appear to be more prone to heart attacks and it was research into the incidence of premature deaths due to heart disease which originally led to the formulation of the Type A/Type B theory, which is still widely accepted as an explanatory model of the incidence of stress.

Some stress is normal, and indeed healthy. The mechanism of adrenalin release is normal and biologically necessary. You may recognize the effects of adrenalin if you have ever narrowly avoided a car accident or experienced feelings of panic – this is the flight or fight stimulus of adrenalin. Yet too much stress over long periods can be dangerous and damaging.

You will have to find your own balance and manage the potential sources of stress in your life. Periods of relaxation and exercise and some variety in your routine are important. All too frequently the task of combining work and study squeezes out these essential activities. This only exacerbates and accelerates stress. If you recognize yourself as Type A and find it difficult to relax and let go of work-related problems these comments have a special meaning. At the beginning of this course various forms of peer support were discussed. Take advice from a colleague and try to understand and manage the causes of stress in your life.

Stress can also be reflected. One stressed individual in a household is likely to increase the stress levels for other members of the family.

Some discipline in your study, work, sleep and patterns of relaxation will help. Some of the work on stress suggests that the inner clocks of the body are involved in stress. A regular routine and adequate sleep allow us to cope better with the demands of work and life in general. Once again we can draw on an earlier exercise for guidance: your analysis of your use of time (in Exercise 2.1) will show whether or not you are achieving a balance here and point the way to activities which might be reduced or abandoned.

Exercise 7.1

Look back to Exercise 2.1 at your use of time during a typical working day and try to identify intervals when you could relax. Can you make time more available for exercise or relaxation?

Managing stress using SWOT

A very simple management tool gives us an easy way of identifying ways in which you manage stress at present and points to risk areas and opportunities for improving things. SWOT analysis (Strengths, Weaknesses, Opportunities and Threats) is a simple device. Try Exercise 7.2.

Exercise 7.2

SWOT and stress

Draw up a simple grid plan with headings Strengths, Weaknesses, Opportunities and Threats, and try to list under each heading activities and features which describe you. Use the table to check through your lifestyle and identify areas where your hobbies, sports or occupation give you a way of relaxing or exercising – strengths. Next work through those situations in which you feel exposed to stress and where you might make changes – weaknesses. Then turn to opportunities which you may have for taking more exercise, relaxing or changing the way in which you work or study. Finally, try to think of features and aspects of your lifestyle which expose you to undue stress – the threats. Are you in a high stress rated occupational group? Are there features of your diet or lifestyle which could be changed?

Examinations and stress

Your decision to take up a management course almost invariably means that at some stage you will have to sit examinations, unless of course you opt for those short courses which are not examined. However, most college and business school courses leading to diplomas and degrees involve the dreaded three-hour written examination. For many of us this is an unwelcome and stressful hurdle. What can be done to reduce the stress associated with such events?

The steps can be broken down into four stages.

1. Careful course work and note-taking: this clears the way and prepares your study notes for the revision period.
2. Revision planned and carried out ahead of time, to a schedule.
3. A final schedule which includes sleep and relaxation.
4. A plan for tackling each examination paper.

Some stress will occur prior to and during an examination. You need to recognize and accept this from the beginning, but equally you need to be adequately prepared so that extra energy and concentration are channelled into the exam itself.

Some colleges and some distance learning bodies, such as the Open University, have introduced exam counselling sessions to reduce pre-exam anxiety, which for some people can be debilitating and harmful. If you recognize yourself as suffering from this extreme form of exam nerves then these sessions are for you, and if such sessions are not available medical help may be advisable. Otherwise some commonsense advice can serve adequately, giving us the planned strategy:

1. *Plan ahead*: take time off work for revision if possible (some companies will allow a week off for examination preparation) and use the time:
   (a) to revise your course work systematically; and
   (b) to try out sample examination questions against the clock.
2. *Sleep, exercise and relaxation* immediately beforehand will all help to put you in the right balanced frame of mind for the big day.

If this advice clearly does not fit you, another course of action is open to you – this we can call the 'cramming strategy'. First, you should try to ensure that you get enough sleep and a good diet in the run-up to the examination and that you attempt some parts of a planned revision strategy; but at the same time accept that you will need and want to work right up to the last minute. Here the intention is to ensure that you are able to keep going through the examination period, with the promise to yourself of some rest and relaxation afterwards.

Summary

The mechanisms which we associate with stress are a normal part of our physiology enabling us to react quickly to danger. Stress is a condition in which the body is constantly responding in this way to stimuli. The symptoms of stress include fatigue, irritability and poor performance.

As a manager you should be aware of stress as an occupational hazard for you and for those around you in the workplace. Any decision to return to formal study on a part-time basis while working as a manager will increase the likelihood of stress for you, a position which must be considered and then managed. Full-time study in mid-career is likely to carry with it some financial burdens, another source of stress.

This book is concerned with study skills to help you perform more effectively as a management student, but be aware of stress and its dangers and take steps to manage the stress in your life.

8
Conclusion: Over to You –
Continuing the Development
of Your Study Skills

This book has introduced and discussed a range of important skills which you need to acquire in order to enjoy and gain the greatest benefits from any management course, whether full or part time. After an initial period of doubt and apprehension most managers find the return to learning fun and stimulating. In any course with face-to-face teaching much of the work is done in a small groups. Such a study group provides a secure setting in which to test and experiment with ideas. The risks of failure are low and there is a great deal to be learned from other students. This position is also recognized by the designers of distance learning management courses, where you will find that the provision of weekend residential schools and similar arrangements ensures that managers taking these courses also enjoy and gain from the benefits of working in teams and groups.

Many people embark on a management career without any formal training either in management or in its component subject areas. Fortunately, most medium to large companies now offer a variety of short courses varying in duration from one or two days to a week or more. In some, these form a coherent programme, but rarely lead to any qualification which can be recognized by other potential employers. Recently, some major concerns such as IBM, British Airways and the Burton Group have started to set up 'in-company' MBA programmes in conjunction with universities in the United Kingdom. Schemes such as these and the general expansion in management education are changing the face of training. The increased rates of change and the pressures of competition are the driving forces for these shifts, but their net effect is to increase the need for all managers to have a degree of competence in study skills.

The content of many in-company short courses is inevitably focused on the immediate needs of the company and their virtue is a strong practical orientation. Courses at this level make only a limited demand on the learning skills considered in this book. At a mid and senior level the orientation and content of management training change. It becomes more abstract and examines theories and concepts which explain the behaviour of organizations and their interactions with the commercial and governmental environment. In some senses this form of training is more demanding. There is more reading, report-writing and debate. This reflects the nature of many senior management jobs, where less time is spent on operations management and more time is spent thinking about and planning the future of the organization. Not only will a senior manager find more and more reports coming across his or her desk but the time spent in meetings increases and new communication skills are needed.

Report-writing and communication skills are the other side of this particular coin, so the study skills discussed here have another direct application to work.

The development of effective study skills relies on practice and experience. Both will yield an invisible return in the form of a growing self-confidence and the ability to tackle new ideas and new areas of work. We hope that you will use the exercises in this book to revise and improve your skills. They can be repeated at will or simply transferred and applied to other examples taken from your own experience. Planning and managing change are and will remain crucial to today's manager, but this must start with the changes you want to bring about for yourself. Your formal study programme will make its own demands but can also be used to develop further and improve your study skills if you are prepared to apply the lessons contained in these pages. Try to stand back and examine your progress. This book has been written to help you to be self-aware and self-critical of study skills. Finally, remember that you alone are responsible for your use of study time – manager manage yourself – good luck!

References and Further Reading

Adams, J. L (1988) *The Care and Feeding of Ideas*, Penguin, London.

Buzan, T. (1974) *Use your Head*, BBC, London.

Capel, I. and Gurnsey, J. (1987) *Managing Stress*, Constable, London.

Constable, J. and McCormick, R. (1987) *The Making of British Managers*, British Institute of Management/MSC/NEDO, London.

Cooper, L., Cooper, R. D. and Eaker, L. H. (1988) *Living with Stress*, Penguin, London.

Freeman, R. (1986) *Mastering Study Skills*, Macmillan, London

Gower, E. (1971) *The Complete Plain Words*, Penguin, London

Handy, C. (1987) *The Making of Managers*, NEDO, London.

Hanson, P. (1986) *The Joy of Stress*, Pan, London.

HMSO (1987) *Understanding Stress*, Parts 1, 2 and 3, HMSO, London.

Maddox, H. (1988) *How to Study*, revised edn, Pan, London.

Marshall, L. and Rowland, F. (1983) *A Guide to Learning Independently*, Open University Press, Milton Keynes.

National Extension College/Lucas (1985) *How to Work Effectively*, National Extension College, Cambridge.

Open University (1984) *Plain English* (T101 supplementary material), Open University Press, Milton Keynes.

Oxford University Press (1984) *The Oxford Guide to the English Language*, Oxford University Press.

Peters, T. and Waterman, R. (1982) *In Search of Excellence*, Harper & Row, London.

Rowntree, D. (1988) *Learn how to Study*, Macdonald Orbis, London.
Wheatley, D. (1988) *Report Writing*, Penguin, London.
Williams, L. V. (1986) *Teaching for the Two-Sided Mind*, Touchstone/Simon & Schuster, New York.

Index